AGAINST
COMMON SENSE

The phrase "teaching for social justice" is often used, but not always explained. What does it really mean to teach for social justice? What are the implications for anti-oppressive teaching across different areas of the curriculum? Drawing on his own experiences teaching diverse grades and subjects, Kevin K. Kumashiro examines various aspects of anti-oppressive teaching and learning in six different subject areas. Connecting practice to theory through new pedagogical elements, the revised edition of this bestselling text features:

- A new and timely preface that considers the possibilities of anti-oppressive teaching and teaching for social justice in the face of increasing pressure from both the Right and the Left to accept neoliberal school reform policies.
- End-of-chapter questions that enhance comprehension of arguments, help concretize abstract ideas into classroom practice, and encourage critique.
- A sampling of print and online resources that will inspire students to further their social justice education.

The new pedagogical components of the revised edition of *Against Common Sense* will offer K-12 teachers and teacher educators the tools they need to teach against their common-sense assumptions and continue the evolution of social justice in education.

Kevin K. Kumashiro is an Associate Professor and Chair of Educational Policy Studies at the University of Illinois-Chicago.

AGAINST COMMON SENSE

Teaching and Learning Toward Social Justice

Revised Edition

Kevin K. Kumashiro

Foreword by Gloria Ladson-Billings
Afterword by William F. Pinar

Routledge
Taylor & Francis Group

NEW YORK AND LONDON

First edition published 2004
by RoutledgeFalmer
270 Madison Ave, New York, NY 10016

This edition published 2009
by Routledge
270 Madison Ave, New York, NY 10016

Simultaneously published in the UK
by Routledge
2 Park Square, Milton Park, Abingdon, Oxon OX14 4RN

Routledge is an imprint of the Taylor & Francis Group, an informa business

Printed and bound in the United States of America on acid-free paper by
Walsworth Publishing Company, Marceline, MO

Library of Congress Cataloging-in-Publication Data
Kumashiro, Kevin K., 1970–
    Against common sense : teaching and learning toward social justice / Kevin K.
Kumashiro.—2nd ed.
        p.cm.—(Reconstructing the public sphere in curriculum studies)
Includes bibliographical references.
    1. Educational equalization—United States.   2. Social justice—Study and teaching—
United States.   3. Teachers—Training of—United States.   I. Title.
    LC213.2.K86 2009
        370.11'5—dc22   2009012020

ISBN 10: 0–415–80221–0 (hbk)
ISBN 10: 0–415–80222–9 (pbk)
ISBN 10: 0–203–87006–9 (ebk)

ISBN 13: 978–0–415–80221–5 (hbk)
ISBN 13: 978–0–415–80222–2 (pbk)
ISBN 13: 978–0–203–87006–8 (ebk)

To all educators who,
often at great risk,
teach against oppression.

TABLE OF CONTENTS

ACKNOWLEDGMENTS TO
THE REVISED EDITION

Thank you to Catherine Bernard and the many staff at Routledge for encouraging me to update this book. This second edition would not have been possible without the ongoing support and mentorship of Vicki Chou, Bill Ayers, Carl Grant, Christine Sleeter, Erica Meiners, and Therese Quinn. The reflection questions and new resources resulted from discussions with my students, Franklin Chang, Kay Fujiyoshi, Tony Speed, and especially Jung Kim, as well as friends of the Center for Anti-Oppressive Education. Perhaps most important, thank you to all of the educators and activists who have used the first edition of this book, and in the process, allowed me to support and learn from the important work being done in schools and universities across the nation and the world.

ACKNOWLEDGMENTS

Anti-oppressive education is difficult to research and practice. I began this book at a time when those difficulties overwhelmed my sense of self and my confidence in being able to make a difference for the students and teachers in our schools. Yet, many people have entered my life in ways that enabled me to continue this work, and I hope they will view this acknowledgment as but a small token of my appreciation.

This book builds on my earlier research, activism, and teaching experiences, and I thank the many people who offered guidance, collegiality, and technical expertise in such efforts. I know I am failing to list everyone who should be listed, but as a starter: Stacey Lee, Elizabeth Ellsworth, Carl Grant, Monica Serrano, Joy Lei, Bic Ngo, Ann Schulte, Bill Tierney, Jim Sears, Eric Rofes, my colleagues from Bates College, my collaborators in previous publications, and my comrades in GLSEN-Southern Maine and other activist organizations.

As I drafted and redrafted this book, I turned to friends who shared with me an incredible amount of their time and insights to help me clarify and expand and complicate my ideas and arguments and examples: Lisa Loutzenheiser, Tom Robertson, Patrick Slattery, Lisa Smulyan, and especially Eric Collum. Although I take responsibility for errors and gaps, I know that this book has become one of which I can be proud because of their assistance. Thank you!

I thank Gloria Ladson-Billings and Bill Pinar for generously and graciously writing the Foreword and Afterword to this book. Their shared insights and personal reflections urge us all to complicate my ideas and strive harder to do this work. I am especially grateful that they took time out of schedules filled with deadlines and life hardships to contribute to my book—they model what it means to support emerging scholars, and I hope I can do for others what they have done for me.

I thank the staff at RoutledgeFalmer for making the publication of this book possible, and I am grateful that Bill Pinar is including this book in his exciting new book series.

Finally, I thank the many people who have helped to make possible who I have become and who I am becoming, including my family, my former teachers and students, my friends, my colleagues, and the many anti-oppressive educators, activists, and researchers who are making our schools and society better places for all. We have much more to do, and we should remember that we are not alone.

ABOUT THE AUTHOR

Kevin K. Kumashiro, Ph.D., is the founding director of the Center for Anti-Oppressive Education (http://antioppressiveeducation.org) where he develops resources for members of educational communities interested in creating and engaging in anti-oppressive forms of education. He has worked as a teacher and teacher educator in public and private schools and colleges in the United States and abroad, and has served as a consultant for various schools, school districts, and state and federal agencies. His previous books include *Troubling Intersections of Race and Sexuality* (Rowman & Littlefield, 2001), *Troubling Education* (RoutledgeFalmer, 2002), and *Restoried Selves* (Haworth, 2003).

FOREWORD

Writing a foreword always gives me pause. One never wants to "oversell" a volume by writing a foreword that promises more than the author(s)/editor(s) intends. On the contrary, one never wants to write in ways that diminish the volume's contribution. In this foreword my words, if not totally accurate, are at least comfortable because Kevin Kumashiro takes up a topic near and dear to me—preparing teachers to teach in ways that disrupt, challenge, work against, and critique the status quo. This teaching is based on an assumption that something is very wrong with our current social order and that the regular and predictable failure of students based on race, class, and/or gender must be challenged. Few people will deny the facts of the assumption or the nobility of the goal. However, how teachers mount these challenges remains contested. Two recent incidents are illustrative.

During a routine observation of one of my Teaching Assistant's classes, I was struck by the resistance of several of his students to his pleas to teach for social justice. One of his students, who was himself a student of color, challenged the notion that he should be preparing students to change society. This student insisted that his job as a teacher was to help students "feel good about themselves" and to experience as much success as possible in his classroom. Later that day I ran into the student in the corridor and we continued the conversation. The student felt it was "unfair" of the teacher education program to expect teachers to change the world and emphasized that all he wanted to do was to teach the students in his classroom. The young man and I spent about twenty minutes discussing the goals and focus of the university's teacher education program and the fact that many of the faculty members who comprised our department had deep and long-standing commitments to teaching as a way to change society. The longer we talked the clearer it became to me that the young man was not opposed to social justice. Rather, he was overwhelmed by the demands of a teacher education program that seemed to require him to teach students basic skills (e.g., reading, writing, and mathematics), prepare them for the information age (e.g., through science and technology), and ensure that they lived productive and enjoyable lives (e.g., through social studies, art, music, and physical education). When was he going to have time to "save the world"?

A second incident that came to mind as I read this volume occurred during a doctoral dissertation oral defense. The student had conducted a study where he examined the practice of young teachers of color who were (in the student's words) "teaching for change." In the midst of the oral, one of the examiners argued that the teachers were not acting as change agents and challenged the doctoral candidate to provide evidence that they were. In exasperation the examinee argued, "I know the critical theorists and post moderns think that teachers should be doing all manner of things, but most teachers are just trying to survive the school day. The changes that these teachers made in their curriculum, in their pedagogy, and in their interactions with students and their families represent real change and may be all that is possible in REAL classrooms."

Both of these incidents remind me that we all have ideal notions of what teachers are and should be. But ideal notions are just that—ideals. The real work of teaching is messy and complex. It does not conform to the neat conceptions of anti-racist, anti-sexist, anti-homophobic, anti-oppressive education about which we theorize. In this volume, Kumashiro explores the challenges of anti-oppressive pedagogy along with concrete examples of viable classroom solutions. This work is reminiscent of two well-known pieces of literature published in the *Harvard Educational Review,* one by Timothy Lensmire, entitled "Writing Workshop as Carnival: Reflections on an Alternative Learning Environment" and the other by Paul Skilton Sylvester, entitled "Elementary School Curricula and Urban Transformation." Lensmire argues that no matter how enamored we become with a pedagogy (in this case, writing workshop), we have to be careful that the pedagogy actually meets students' academic needs along with our perceived pedagogical ones. Sylvester illustrates the ways that students' everyday experiences can be recruited as the basis for curriculum transformation. Both articles focus on the limits and possibilities of the classroom. Like my frustrated teacher education student and the exasperated doctoral candidate, the authors point to just what can (and perhaps cannot) be done in the classroom.

Yet, the fact that the classroom is fraught with challenges and constraints is not an excuse for failing to grapple with social justice issues and anti-oppressive pedagogies. Rather, these challenges and constraints help us understand the dimensions and contours of our practices. When I began teaching I was assigned to a working-class, White ethnic community. My students were from Italian American, Polish American, Irish American, and Jewish American families (with a group of African Americans bussed in from across town). The major issues concerning my students and their families were adequate food, clothing, and shelter. Many of the fathers were union laborers—longshoremen who belonged to the Teamsters. I could spend many classroom sessions talking about the American labor movement and the exploitation of U.S. workers. Many parents were eager to share stories of labor strikes and inequity in the workplace.

However, I had to tread lightly over issues of race and gender equity. I was one of three African American teachers in the school. Race relations between African Americans and working-class Whites in South Philadelphia were extremely strained. Many of the parents did not accept me as a teacher. I confess that my decision to soft pedal issues of race and racism was less informed by pedagogical wisdom than concern for my safety. I had no real allies and I had not yet earned tenure. I had no intention of becoming a rebel with a cause but no job.

Sometime in the middle of my first year the father of one of my students died. I took up a collection from the students and teachers in the school and delivered it to the home. The family was Irish American and unbeknownst to me observed a traditional Irish funeral where the wake took place in the family home. I was terrified of dead bodies, and had I known Mr. Doherty would be "present" at the event I would have either mailed the contribution or prevailed upon a colleague to deliver it. Instead, I walked into the house where the deceased was "laid out" and mustered enough courage to stay and console the family. For weeks people in the community talked about the young Black teacher who comforted the Doherty's. I was starting to build an alliance. By the time I left that school, I could teach almost anything I wanted to because I had built a network of trust with the parents and community members. This important first step often is overlooked by new teachers or teachers new to a community.

Teacher educators may arm their prospective teachers with ideological supports and activities to promote an anti-oppressive social justice pedagogy, but they sometimes forget to equip them with the kinds of interpersonal skills that must be mastered in order to garner support for what might be unpopular and politically dangerous curriculum and pedagogical decisions. Do we merely allow them to move ahead in a trial-and-error-like fashion, or do we have an obligation to provide supports that move them more confidently from ideology to pedagogy?

Kevin Kumashiro's *Against Common Sense: Teaching and Learning Toward Social Justice* offers just the type of support teachers need to negotiate the challenges of anti-oppressive teaching. Rather than preach at teachers about what they should do, this volume offers them choices about what they can do. It is filled with specific examples that are rich with context and real-life experiences rather than a formulaic set of prescriptions. It is engaging, challenging, and encouraging. Beyond examples of teaching there are examples of learning. Kumashiro admonishes us that one of our major responsibilities is to learn—to learn from and with students about their lives, their worlds, and the wider world beyond the classroom and school.

Gloria Ladson-Billings
University of Wisconsin-Madison

INTRODUCTION TO THE REVISED EDITION

NEW POLITICAL CONTEXT

It is January 2009, and I find myself reflecting on the inauguration of our new president. Like many others, I prayed that the American people would elect Barack Obama as our next president, and I cried with joy when he won decisively two months ago. "Yes, We Can," he proclaimed, and his election as the United States' first Black president signaled an era of change, of progress, of hope—or at least, the promise of such. Today, mixed with my feelings of hope and anticipation are feelings of grave concern, particularly for our nation's youth. Within weeks of his election, Obama began to nominate his cabinet, including his new Secretary of Education, Arne Duncan. With Obama's inauguration came a swift Senate confirmation of Duncan with nothing but praise for his accomplishments as CEO of the Chicago Public School District for the past seven years. Duncan's accomplishments in Chicago suggest the direction that he will take the nation's public schools. Given that his appointment immediately precedes the anticipated and long-awaited reauthorization of the Elementary and Secondary Education Act (ESEA) (dubbed "No Child Left Behind" under George W. Bush), Duncan's impact on education reform can be widespread and long-lasting.

Duncan's signature initiative in Chicago is Renaissance 2010, an initiative that was launched in 2004 that aimed to open 100 new smaller schools and close about sixty so-called "failing" schools by the year 2010. To date, seventy-five new schools have opened. Many of them are charter schools that serve fewer low-income, limited English-language proficient, and disabled students than regular neighborhood public schools. More than a third of them are in communities that are not high-needs areas. During Duncan's tenure, districtwide high-school test scores have not risen, and most of the lowest performing high schools saw scores drop. Renaissance 2010 is not doing enough to support those students who struggle the most.

This should not be surprising. The blueprint of Renaissance 2010 lies in a report entitled, "Left Behind," produced a year earlier by the Commercial Club of Chicago, which mapped out a strategy for schools to align more closely with the goals of the business elite. Central to that strategy was the creation of 100 new charter schools, managed by for-profit businesses, and freed of Local School Councils and teacher unions—groups that historically have put the welfare of poor and minority students before that of the business sector.

Business leaders have long had influence over America's schools. In the early 1900s, the business sector influenced how large school districts were consolidated and managed. In the late 1900s and into the era of "No Child Left Behind," the Business Roundtable (which currently consists of the top 300 business CEOs in the United States) influenced how policy makers narrowly defined "standards" and "accountability." Today, public debates are framed by business principles, and certain of these assumptions go unquestioned and are considered to be simply "common sense." This includes the assumption that improvement comes when schools are put into competition with one another, like businesses in a so-called free market.

Duncan's initiatives are steeped in a free-market model of school reform, particularly the notion that school choice and 100 new charter and specialty schools will motivate educators to work harder to do better, as will penalties for not meeting standards. But research does not support such initiatives. There is evidence that opening new schools and encouraging choice and competition will not raise districtwide achievement, and charter schools in particular are not outperforming regular schools. There is evidence that choice programs actually exacerbate racial segregation. And there is evidence that high-stakes testing actually increases the dropout rate.

What is significant, here, is that Duncan's initiatives fit a larger movement to reform public schools that has been shaped by pro-business and conservative forces in the United States. For the past few decades, education reform has been increasingly influenced by conservative, neoliberal, and Christian fundamentalist organizations (what I am collectively calling the political Right) in initiatives such as choice programs, standards and testing movements, censored curriculums, policies that limit spending, policies that hinder labor organizing, alternative fast-track teacher and administrator certifications, and so on. One way that the Right has been successful in changing education policy is through strategic messages that influence or frame what the general public takes to be "common sense" about what schools should look like and how schools should be reformed. In fact, the Right has become so successful at framing the debate as to influence even those organizations that have historically been associated with the political Left, resulting in initiatives—such as those regarding school safety and closing the achievement gaps—by "liberal" organizations that indirectly coincide with the goals of the Right. In this way, Duncan's appointment signals the extent to which even Obama's administration has been swayed by neoliberal framings of education reform.

"Standards" is another example of a Rightist frame that is embraced by both Republicans and Democrats. In January 2002, President Bush signed into law the No Child Left Behind (NCLB) Act, which reauthorized the Elementary and Secondary Education Act and instituted changes that both Democrats and Republicans were calling the most substantial since the law's creation in 1965. Although credited to the Bush Administration, NCLA had wide bipartisan support and was co-sponsored by one of the more senior and liberal members of the Democratic Party, Senator Edward Kennedy.

Important to note is that NCLB did not originate with the Bush Administration. Much of the framework for NCLB was developed in the final years of the Clinton Administration under Democratic appointees and staff. Although some of the details of NCLB changed with the change of administration, several central concepts or frames remained intact. In fact, in the presidential campaigns of subsequent Democratic candidates (Al Gore in 2000, John Kerry in 2004, and Barack Obama in 2008), the public heard proposals that may have differed from NCLB in the details, but that remained within four central frames:

- *Standards*: We need to have high standards for students, teachers, and schools.
- *Accountability*: We need to hold students, teachers, and schools accountable for reaching those standards and demonstrating that they did so on such measures as standardized tests.
- *Sanctions and rewards*: There will be sanctions for not meeting those standards and rewards for doing so.

- *Choice*: In those schools that do not meet standards, parents should have the choice to move their children elsewhere.

These frames, especially regarding standards and testing, trace back to even before the Clinton Administration. Although the 1994 reauthorization of ESEA during the Clinton Administration required states to develop content and performance standards and created the notion of "adequate yearly progress," it was the early years of the Reagan Administration and the release of its report, *A Nation at Risk,* that signaled the beginning of a standards-and-testing movement that has spanned the past quarter century and culminates in NCLB. Education reform has been framed by the language of standards and testing for almost three decades from both political parties as well as in individual schools districts across the nation. The Chicago Public School District, for example, influenced Clinton's vision of education reform in the mid-1990s by providing what he called "a model for the nation" in terms of standards, high-stakes testing, school accountability, and centralized regulation of teachers and schools. From both Republicans and Democrats, proposals for education reform have come to be shaped by the same concepts, thus reinforcing the notion that these concepts are the way things should be, are given, are merely "common sense."

Of course, many people on the Left are critical of current ways of thinking about standards. However, a common mistake by many of the Left is to create a false division between social-justice education and standards-based reforms. Don't get me wrong—I believe that there is much reason for concern over the increasing heightened emphasis on curriculum or learning "standards." As many other scholars have argued, curriculum standards reflect what some in society believe are the things that students should know and be able to do, and thus cannot help but reflect only certain perspectives and advance only certain goals. Any iteration of standards is a necessarily partial story of whatever topic is being learned, and can function to privilege not only certain perspectives, but also certain groups in society.

The notion that curriculum can reinforce social hierarchies was insightfully made nearly a century ago by Carter G. Woodson who, in his *Miseducation of the Negro,* argued that schools indirectly teach students to fit into a White-dominated racial hierarchy by developing in them a particular *racial consciousness.* Parallel arguments have been made many times since, regarding other social hierarchies, including feminist critiques of how schools teach a particular gender consciousness, neo-Marxist critiques of social-class consciousness, queer critiques of sexuality consciousness, and post-colonial critiques of nationhood consciousness.

But having such concerns about curriculum does not mean that we should reject all use of curriculum standards. Such a move is self-defeating, given the growing movements nationally and internationally towards standards-based reforms. Currently, schools and educators have little choice but to teach towards standards, or risk school closure, teacher turnover, student non-promotion, and other repercussions. In addition, and perhaps more important, such a move limits our ability to engage in social justice education.

Teaching towards social justice does not mean teaching the "better" curriculum or the better story; rather, it means teaching students to think independently, critically, and creatively about whatever story is being taught, whether that is the dominant narrative or any number of alternative perspectives from the margins. Furthermore, teaching towards social justice involves preparing students to succeed in whatever context they find themselves, including contexts that privilege and value the dominant narratives, the mainstream culture, the "traditional values," and the rules for succeeding that often are unspoken and taken-for-granted. Curriculum standards are one way that schools can make such rules explicit and accessible. Therefore, while schools should not uncritically teach to standards, it is also the case that schools should not reject curriculum standards as antithetical to social justice education. Rather, schools should use standards in paradoxical ways, namely, by teaching students to reach them but simultaneously supporting students in seeing where and how the standards have gaps, where they include and exclude certain perspectives and experiences, advance certain goals, privilege certain groups, and so on.

The refusal to define social justice education in opposition to Rightist initiatives in education is central to what I am arguing should be a priority of not only the Left, but of all who care about the quality of education and the quality of life of our nation's youth. Partial standards and curriculum materials should be seen as the necessary substance of social justice education. Indeed, we might view social justice education as that which happens only what we are presented with such materials, only when we are surrounded by such requirements and demands, and only when we ourselves are still struggling with questions about the "what else," "how else," and "where else" that are involved in such teaching. Social justice education requires grappling with paradox, with partiality, and with the uncertainty and discomfort that often accompany such commitments.

Increasingly, I meet brilliant young activists who choose not to go into teaching because they do not see how, in today's schools, it is possible to be a teacher-activist. Among my colleagues and friends and relatives who are veteran teachers, I see more and more leaving the profession for much the same reason. The challenges are daunting: the pressure to teach to the test, the narrowing and even scripting of curriculum, the increasing professional demands and public criticism, the heightened monitoring and censoring of anything or anyone deemed too "political" (that is, too willing to question the status quo or the powers that be), and the muting of teacher voices in school governance and education reform. Now more than ever, we need to redefine what it means to be a teacher, so that activism becomes a central part of that identity. We need to reshape how we prepare and support teachers in contexts that actively hinder social justice education. We need to reconceptualize social justice education so that it explicitly responds to and even capitalizes on the ways that the Right has come to dominate schools.

This context provides all the more reason for me to revise this book. As I was recently reminded by a friend and mentor: progressive change happens not merely when a strong individual assumes a position of leadership, but more importantly, when each one of us assumes the responsibility to lead, to take action, to build movement. Social justice in education is needed now. And every educator—at every grade level in every subject area—has a role to play.

In this revised edition of *Against Common Sense*, I have added questions at the end of each chapter to spark personal reflections and, when used with a group of educators, to guide classroom discussion. Each set includes questions to enhance *comprehension* of the arguments, to help *concretize* the abstract ideas into classroom practice, and to encourage *critique* or expansion that invites ideas beyond what was presented in the book. I have also added a sampling of print and online resources that have become available since I first wrote this book. These books and websites both illustrate and expand on my arguments in this book, which is particularly important and useful when recognizing that this book includes only some examples of what it means to apply these ideas in one's own teaching and learning.

Much more work remains to be done. But we have much more available to us to build on. I hope that this revised edition is helpful in this important and urgent work, and I urge you to invite many more people to join us as we teach and learn towards social justice.

SAMPLING OF NEW RESOURCES

For analyses of the influence of the Right on U.S. education, teacher education, educational policy, and education around the world:

- Groenke, S. L., & Hatch, J. A. (Eds.). (2009). *Critical Pedagogy and Teacher Education in the Neoliberal Era: Small Openings.* London: Springer.
- Kumashiro, K. K. (2008). *The Seduction of Common Sense: How the Right Has Framed the Debate on America's Schools.* New York: Teachers College Press.
- McCarthy, C., & Teasley, C. (Eds.). (2008). *Transnational Perspectives on Culture, Policy, and Education: Redirecting Cultural Studies in Neoliberal Times.* New York: Peter Lang.
- Shaker, P., & Heilman, E. E. (2008). *Reclaiming Education for Democracy: Thinking Beyond No Child Left Behind.* New York: Routledge.

INTRODUCTION

THE PROBLEM OF COMMON SENSE

I began my teaching career as did many others: I wanted to "help." Fresh out of college, I had conscientiously searched for a teaching job that reflected my save-the-world idealism, and found no better opportunity than that offered by the American Peace Corps to be a teacher in Nepal. Along with thirty other Volunteers, my transition from student to teacher involved traveling halfway around the world to a society and a school that barely resembled those in which I grew up. I assumed that these schools and people desperately needed our help.

After three months of studying the Nepali language, aspects of Nepali cultures, and different methods of instruction and curriculum design, I headed to my assigned post in a small village in the eastern region of the country. From the end of the bus line my village was a fifty-minute walk on a dirt road that ran alongside the otherwise green hills. The center of the village was the bazaar, or the group of ten or so shops that lined one strip of the road. I rented a room above one of those shops from a family wealthy enough to build a house from wood instead of mud. An additional fifteen minutes uphill on a footpath took me to the school where I was to teach.

As the first few weeks passed, my neighbors taught me much about the facets of life in the village that many of them seemed to take for granted as "common sense" or what everyone should know. I was accustomed to eating a breakfast, lunch, and dinner, but learned that only two meals were served in the shops—one at a little before 10:00 in the morning and another at 5:00 or 6:00 in the evening—with tea at 1:00 in the afternoon. I sometimes cooked my own meals with creative and not always successful attempts at adding more "American" dishes to my diet, but because I was not cooking the rice–lentils–veggie combo that was a staple of Nepali meals, my neighbors said that I did not know how to cook. I was obsessed with keeping things clean, but learned that there was only one faucet, located in the center of the bazaar, that was used for different purposes at different times of the day. It served as a shower for groups of men and then groups of women at sunrise, as a dishwasher later in the morning, then as a laundry, then as a dishwasher again, and in the evening, if water was still running, as a source to fill large jugs that could be taken back to one's house. Of course, these routine activities of village life were carried out for good reasons, but without knowing how people generally lived their lives, and without being a part of the life of this village, it took time to change how I thought about meals, water, time, privacy, and other aspects of daily life in Nepal.

Like life in the village, at first life at the school was equally disconcerting, and it similarly took me time to learn what to others was simply common sense. I had prepared long-term plans for my classes, anxious for the first day of school, only to find myself confused when the school officially opened in mid-February but did not begin instruction until late February, when "enough" of the students were attending. I wanted to seat students in mixed-gender groups, but learned that boys had always sat together on one side of the room, girls on the other, and that, further, they preferred this closeness to peers of their same gender because they had to squeeze, in groups of five or six, on benches that spanned barely 4 feet. I tried to manage the classroom with dialogue and verbal admonitions but was often told by students that controlling a classroom meant hitting those who misbehaved. Some students encouraged me to do so. One student even brought a big stick for me to use if classmates got too noisy. I invited students to participate actively in their learning, engage in discussion, talk to one another, and address problems collaboratively, but confronted a tendency, even a desire among many students to sit quietly, copy exactly what was written on the board, and respond to me verbally only as a group.

Perhaps most significantly, I had wanted to introduce activities and materials and problems to solve that I had created on my own, but I learned that class lessons had always centered directly on the official textbooks, issued by the government and common to all schools in Nepal. The textbooks consisted of sections with sample exercises for teachers to solve in lectures and with parallel practice problems for students to complete as homework. Each day, teachers would begin class with a review of some of the previous night's homework and then proceed to the next section of the textbook, lecturing on the solutions to the sample problems, which students were to mimic that night as they completed the practice problems. Typically, classes covered one section per day, which was the pace necessary to complete the entire book in time for the end-of-year standardized tests. Produced by the government and containing problems almost identical to those presented in the textbooks, these tests determined whether students would move to the next grade level.

Early on, some of my students asked me not to spend time on work that was not in the textbook. Some students would show me completed homework from the next section in the book that I had not yet assigned, asking me to please follow the sequence and do what we were "supposed" to be doing. Some students laughed, thinking I was joking, when I said that their grades would be determined not only by the midterm and end-of-year exams (which was how grades had always been determined), but also by homework and projects. Some students even complained to the other teachers, worried that I was jeopardizing their chances of passing the end-of-year exams because I was not "teaching." My classes might have been "fun" and I might have been "nice," but I was certainly not doing what teachers were supposed to be doing and that was a problem.

It seemed that students and faculty already had clear ideas about what it meant to teach and learn, and my attempts to teach differently simply did not make sense. Of course, getting students and teachers to think differently about what it means to teach was exactly why I was sent there. My assignment as a Resource Teacher was to introduce schools to different and presumably more effective ways to teach, to help the teachers to question their perspectives and practices, and then integrate some of the teaching methods that I had experienced in my youth. The lecture–practice–exam approach to teaching had become so ingrained in the practices of Nepal's schools as to have become a part of "common sense." Such an approach did not conform to what I had been taught was sound pedagogy. As someone who experienced a different form of education in the United States, I brought different assumptions, expectations, and values to the school. It was easy for me, as an outsider looking in, to raise questions about the purpose or effectiveness of many of these practices.

Ironically, the Peace Corps was not acting much differently than were my students. Like my students, the Peace Corps relied on a commonsensical definition of good teaching that was informed primarily by how teaching was generally experienced, discussed, and conceptualized in the United States. After all, beyond the few hours of teacher education that we received before heading to our posts, most of the Peace Corps Volunteers had received little or no preparation to be teachers, and most of us had had very little teaching experience before joining the Peace Corps. Yet, we were told that we were all capable of serving as Resource Teachers because we had had over sixteen years' experience as students in the U.S. educational system. Good teaching was not something that we needed to learn; rather, it was something we had already learned.

One reason that I and, I imagine, my Peace Corps colleagues embraced the idea that the "American way" was both better than the "Nepali way" and applicable in Nepali contexts was the apparent similarity between practices in Nepali schools and practices we had just learned were outdated in the United States. Our training in curriculum and instruction had suggested that more and more U.S. teachers were moving away from models of teaching that emphasized lecture–practice–exams as they implemented approaches that, research suggested, were more effective in increasing student engagement and learning. By implication, our training had suggested that instruction in Nepali schools was akin to instruction in U.S. schools several decades ago. With our help, Nepali teachers could catch up to their U.S. counterparts.

I am not suggesting that exposing teachers to different teaching methods was itself problematic. On the contrary, I think learning different methods is essential to improving as a teacher. What was problematic was our failure to critique our unspoken assumptions about U.S. superiority. And perhaps a more significant problem was our failure to unearth the ways that U.S. values and priorities and ideologies were embedded in our approaches to teaching and learning. As I will argue throughout this book, embedded in any way of thinking about teaching and learning are values and perspectives, including values and perspectives that can be quite oppressive (i.e., that privilege or favor certain ways of being in this world and marginalize or disadvantage others). What have come to be defined as good teaching in the United States are approaches to teaching that reinforce certain ways of thinking, of identifying, and of relating to others, including ways that comply with different forms of oppression (including racism, sexism, classism, heterosexism, colonialism, and other "isms"). "Good teaching" is not a neutral concept.

So, our stated goal may have been to share with schools in Nepal some of what had become common sense in the United States, namely, that teaching should consist of more than lectures, rote memorization, textbooks, and tests. But at an unspoken level, our goal was also to help schools in Nepal adopt what many in the United States have learned about teaching and, in essence, be more like "American" schools. Our goal was to help teachers to think of teaching as many in the United States think of teaching, and to help students experience learning as we have experienced learning. In this way, the Peace Corps was engaging in a form of cultural imperialism, teaching "them" to value and become more like "us."

We in the Peace Corps were not taught to examine how importing "American ways" of teaching could simultaneously privilege certain ways of thinking about education, knowledge, progress, or the world, especially ways that favor the United States or only certain racial or cultural groups in the world. We were not expected to unravel and complicate our own commonsensical views of education. I, for one, did not question whether an outsider looking at my own taken-for-granted perspectives on what it means to teach would find them strange or unreasonable, or for that matter, oppressive.

COMMON SENSE IN U.S. SCHOOLS

As is the case in Nepal, many aspects of schooling in the United States have become so routine and commonplace that they often go unquestioned. Across the nation and for both young children and adolescents, schools generally open from early morning until mid-afternoon, Monday through Friday, from the end of summer until the beginning of the next summer. Students spend most of their time studying the four "core disciplines" of social studies, English language and literature, the natural sciences, and mathematics. Less frequently in elementary and middle schools and often as electives in secondary schools, students also study such disciplines as foreign languages (or languages other than English), physical education, the arts, and vocational education.

At both elementary and secondary levels, classes in each subject generally last between one and two hours, meet every day or every other day, and consist of one teacher, perhaps an adult assistant, and a group of about ten, twenty, thirty, maybe forty students. Students are usually grouped by age, sometimes by gender, and often by abilities (placed into "honors" tracks, for instance, or in classes for those with learning "disabilities" or limited English-language skills). Teaching and learning activities usually take place in a four-walled room where students sit for most of the period, working out of shared books or writing on shared topics or engaging in shared experiments. Teachers are expected to know more than the students, determine what students are supposed to learn, structure the class in such a way that students learn what they are supposed to learn, and then assess whether they learned it with exams or assignments. Students are expected to follow instructions, work hard, and do homework in order to learn what they are supposed to learn; the grade, score, or rank with which they end is meant to reflect the degree to which they succeeded.

Some schools have designed alternative ways to schedule classes, organize the curriculum, and group students, as well as alternative types of activities, evaluations, and goals. The ways we traditionally think about teaching and learning are not the only possible ways. Research has helped to trouble popular notions of what schools are "supposed" to look like. While some people believe that schools have become distracted with social or political issues and instead should be neutral as they focus on academic matters—on the "three Rs" of reading, writing, and arithmetic—research suggests that moral and social issues constantly arise whether or not teachers intend to address them. While some people assert that research has proven certain teaching methods to be most effective and that schools should use these "best practices," researchers disagree about what it is that research actually proves. While some people assume that schools will improve when they are held accountable for teaching certain standards of knowledge and skills, research suggests that disagreement exists over what such standards should consist of and whether current standards will challenge social inequities. Furthermore, research suggests that the official views of what and how schools should teach often reflect the perspectives, experiences, and values of only certain people in society, especially those who have traditionally been privileged or currently wield political influence.

Unfortunately, research findings and schooling practices that run counter to commonsensical ideas of what schools are supposed to be doing are often dismissed as biased, as a distraction from the real work of schools, as inappropriate for schools, or simply as nonsensical. This dismissal seems to be the case among policy makers who are leading the current movements to improve schools through standards, high-stakes tests for students, and repercussions for "failing" schools, as when they continue to call for traditional or neutral forms of knowledge and proven or accountable methods of teaching. What is significant here is not merely the existence of competing views of education, but the insidious ways that they are silenced. Common sense limits what is considered to be consistent with the purposes of schooling. Alternative perspectives, including perspectives that challenge common sense, are *already* dismissed as irrelevant, inconsequential, or inappropriate. After all, common sense does not tell us that this is what schools could be doing; it tells us that this and only this is what schools *should* be doing. This moral imperative ("should") helps to explain why we often feel social pressure to conform, as when we tell ourselves, "It's just common sense that schools teach these things and students do those things," lest we be seen as abnormal, senseless, even counterproductive.

There are at least two reasons why challenging the prescriptive nature of commonsensical ideas is difficult. First, it is difficult to recognize those ideas that are prescriptive. We do not often need to be told explicitly, for example, that the curriculum should include these things and not other things. Rather, we learn that the curriculum has "traditionally" consisted of these things. We do not often need to be told that teachers should teach in these ways and not in those ways. Rather, we learn that teachers are "professional" or "effective" when we teach in these ways. In other words, we do not often question certain practices and perspectives because they are masked by or couched in concepts to which we often feel social pressure to conform, including such concepts as tradition, professionalism, morality, and normalcy.

Of course, social pressure is not always needed. A second reason why challenging the prescriptive nature of commonsensical ideas is difficult is that commonsensical ideas often give us some sense of comfort. After all, commonsensical ideas are often what help us to make sense of and feel at ease with the things that get repeated in our everyday lives. We do not often ask, for instance, why schools open from September through June, or why the materials students learn are divided into disciplines, or why students are grouped by age: Common sense tells us that experiencing such things is what it means to be in school. Were we to learn that there are other ways to structure schooling, or that prevailing views of schooling are actually quite oppressive, we might end up feeling quite disoriented or uncertain or even guilty. It is not hard to imagine feeling quite uncomfortable when learning how everyday social processes define only certain people as normal, or how everyday schooling processes track only certain students toward academic success, including ourselves. It is not hard to imagine instances when we resist challenging the status quo.

Ironically, although the status quo may be comforting for its familiarity and for providing a sense of normalcy, it is also quite oppressive.

The norms of schooling, like the norms of society, privilege and benefit some groups and identities while marginalizing and subordinating others on the basis of race, class, gender, sexual orientation, religion, disabilities, language, age, and other social markers. It has become normal, in other words, for instances of religious intolerance, racial discrimination, gender inequity, economic bias, and other forms of oppression to permeate our educational experiences, as when schools include only certain materials, organize them into only certain disciplines, teach them using only certain methods, and treat students in only certain ways. And it has become normal for us to experience oppression without realizing that we are doing so, especially when, as noted earlier, oppression is masked by or couched in concepts that make us think that this is the way things are supposed to be.

What is significant here is the notion that oppression often plays out unrecognized and unchallenged in schools because it has successfully convinced us that schools are neutral, are nonoppressive, and *should not* be taking a stand one way or the other on issues of oppression. Common sense does not often tell us that the status quo is quite oppressive. It does not often tell us that schools are already contributing to oppression. And it rarely tells us that schools need to place a priority on challenging oppression. Instead, common sense often makes it easy to continue teaching and learning in ways that allow the oppressions already in play to continue to play out unchallenged in our schools and society. The insistence that we "use our common sense" is really an insistence that we view things as some in society have traditionally viewed things and want to continue viewing things. Insisting that we use our common sense when reforming schools is really insisting that we continue to privilege only certain perspectives, practices, values, and groups of people. Common sense is not what should shape educational reform or curriculum design; it is what needs to be examined and challenged.

ANTI-OPPRESSIVE EDUCATION

The question for educational reformers is not *whether* schools should be addressing issues of oppression. Schools are always and already addressing oppression, often by reinforcing it or at least allowing it to continue playing out unchallenged, and often without realizing that they are doing so. The question needs to be *how* schools should be differently addressing issues of oppression. And therein lies the reason for re-centering education on issues of social justice, that is, on a social movement against oppression. The problems of common sense call on us to engage in *anti-oppressive* forms of education, i.e., in forms of education that explicitly work against multiple oppressions.

In recent years, educators and researchers have suggested a range of theories of oppression and practices to challenge oppression. Their suggestions can be grouped generally into four overlapping approaches to anti-oppressive education. The first approach focuses on improving the experiences of students who have traditionally been treated in harmful ways and not treated in helpful ways. Researchers in this group recognize that schools are often spaces where harmful interactions and inaction characterize the experiences of certain students. Harm can result from discrimination, harassment, physical and verbal violence, exclusion, and isolation; a failure of school personnel to intervene in such moments or patterns; insufficient instructional resources; and a lack of attention by educators and support staff. To change such conditions, educators need to transform schools into spaces where all students will be safe, addressed, and affirmed. Educators also need to create spaces within schools where students can go for help, support, advocacy, and resources.

The second approach focuses on changing the knowledge that all students have about people in this world who have traditionally been labeled "different." Researchers in this group recognize that students often come to school with harmful, partial knowledge about people from different racial backgrounds, gender identities, religious affiliations, and so forth: Either they know very little, or they know only what is inferred from stereotypes and myths. When schools do not correct this knowledge, they indirectly allow it to persist unchallenged. To change such mis-knowledge, educators need to broaden students' understanding of differences and different groups of people, and they can do so by integrating into the curriculum a richer diversity of experiences, perspectives, and materials.

The third approach focuses on challenging the broader and often invisible dynamics in society that privilege or favor certain groups and identities and marginalize or disadvantage others. Researchers in this group recognize that oppressive social dynamics are often sustained by various social structures and ideologies, including racial hierarchies, gender stereotypes, heterosexist cultural and religious norms, and legal statutes, which play out differently in different contexts. Such dynamics are often difficult to recognize because they have become regarded as merely the way things have always been and are supposed to be. To change such dynamics, educators need to enable students to become aware of, critique, and resist these dynamics, including the ways that the dynamics may be privileging themselves. Educators also need to revise the curriculum of various disciplines in ways that provide ample opportunities for students to critique and challenge the oppression that may already exist within.

The fourth approach addresses reasons why anti-oppressive education is often difficult to practice. Researchers in this group recognize that we often find comfort in the repetition of what is considered to be common sense, despite the fact that commonsensical ideas and practices can be quite oppressive. Researchers also recognize that we often resist engaging with alternative ways to make sense of and interact with the world around us because such changes can confront us with very discomforting knowledge. To invite students to work toward change, educators need to teach students to address their own subconscious desires for learning only certain things and resistances to learning other things. Furthermore, educators need to address their own desires and resistances to teaching and learning certain things, and refuse to place certainty in any one way of teaching and learning.

Clearly, there is not just one approach to anti-oppressive education. The field of anti-oppressive education draws on many activist traditions, crafting links between feminist, critical, multicultural, queer, postcolonial, and other movements toward social justice. Some approaches respond to and build on others, whereas other approaches critique or contradict others. This should not be surprising. Given that any theory or practice has strengths and weaknesses, the field of anti-oppressive education refuses to say that it has found the "best" approach or even an unproblematic approach to teaching toward social justice. Anti-oppressive education constantly turns its lens of analysis inward as it explores ways that its own perspectives and practices make certain changes possible but others, impossible; and it constantly turns its lens outward to explore the insights made possible by perspectives on teaching and learning that have yet to be adequately addressed in the field of education. Anti-oppressive education is premised on the notion that its work is never done.

So, what does this all mean for the classroom? What might it mean to challenge oppression in different disciplines and at different grade levels? And how might we go about preparing teachers to be these kinds of anti-oppressive educators? This book attempts to address these questions. Part I provides a conceptual framework for thinking about anti-oppressive teacher education. Chapter 1 examines three images that seem to embody the type of teacher being produced in teacher education programs in the United States oriented toward social justice, focusing on their oppressive tendencies and anti-oppressive possibilities. Chapters 2–5 explore alternative ideas of who teachers are and can be, and suggest ways that alternative teacher images can make possible new advances in the movement toward social justice, as by addressing crisis, uncertainty, suffering, and activism.

Part II explores the implications of these concepts for six disciplines: social studies, English literature, music, "foreign" languages, natural sciences, and mathematics. Each chapter centers on a lesson for an elementary, secondary, and/or postsecondary audience, and describes different versions of the lesson. The chapters suggest that different approaches to teaching carry different political implications—some that reinforce oppression and others that challenge oppression. The chapters also suggest that each discipline can uniquely contribute to anti-oppressive change. The book concludes with reflections on practical and political barriers to anti-oppressive education and ways to address such barriers.

The concepts and discipline-based examples presented in this book are not meant to be definitive blueprints for anti-oppressive teaching. Rather, they are meant to illustrate how aspects of the theories presented in Part I can be useful when rethinking and redesigning particular moments in our curriculum. Therefore, readers are encouraged to consider not merely how these concepts and examples can be implemented in their classrooms, but also how these concepts and examples are themselves partial and in need of being problematized. It is important to note that these lessons are intentionally simplified to enable a broad range of readers to grapple with the issues, which means that readers have homework to do as they imagine the implications of these ideas for a wider range of audiences (including younger students or students studying more advanced topics). Furthermore, it is important to view these lessons not as recipes that "work" in every context, but as lessons that, like all lessons, play out differently in different contexts. Toward this end, each chapter in Part II concludes with a section titled "Looking Beyond," which suggests contextual factors that can make difficult the success of any of these lessons. Reading this book requires doing the kind of vigilant, ongoing critique that, it is argued, teachers need to do when teaching and students need to do when learning.

I should clarify that "looking beyond" what and how we teach and learn does not mean that we reject everything, nor does it mean that we search for a better approach. Rather, it means that we raise questions about the necessarily partial and political nature of whatever approach we take. It means that we examine how the things that we teach and learn can both reinforce and challenge oppression, or why we teach and learn only certain things in only certain ways, or what might be alternative ways of teaching and learning and their implications for reinforcing and challenging oppression. Such an analysis can make it clear that, although all approaches to teaching and learning may be partial and political, they are not all equally oppressive or equally anti-oppressive. Some approaches clearly do more to address differences, or oppression, or resistance. As I will argue throughout this book, it is when we examine this partial nature of our teaching and learning that we are able to make significantly different movements toward social justice.

Much work lies ahead. We face resistance in many forms. We face constraints at many levels. We face oppression that plays out well beyond our classrooms and that, therefore, will not end simply because we change what and how we teach. Anti-oppressive education is not the panacea. But change is possible. Change is already happening in classrooms throughout the world, and I expect readers will see themselves already doing versions of many of the suggestions I present in this book. What we need, therefore, is a way to prepare teachers to do more of this kind of work. We need to be preparing teachers who desire the kinds of exciting changes that are made possible when we radically change how we teach and learn. There is much reason to have hope. And I hope this book gives us more tools to make anti-oppressive changes possible.

QUESTIONS FOR REFLECTION AND DISCUSSION

1. (Comprehension) What makes something "common sense," and how can "common sense" be a problem?
2. (Concretization) What aspects of U.S. schools and of educational reforms have become commonsensical today?
3. (Critique) What are strengths and weaknesses of the four primary approaches to anti-oppressive education, and what are alternative ways to conceptualize and illustrate anti-oppressive education?

SAMPLING OF NEW RESOURCES

For analyses of diversity and injustice in schools and society:

- Cole, M. (Ed.). (2006). *Education, Equality and Human Rights: Issues of Gender, "Race", Sexuality, Disability and Social Class.* 2nd Edition. New York: Routledge.
- Pascale, C.-M. (2006). *Making Sense of Race, Class, and Gender: Commonsense, Power, and Privilege in the United States.* New York: Routledge.
- Prashad, V. (2008). *The Darker Nations: A People's History of the Third World.* New York: New Press.

For analyses of education that addresses diversity and injustice:

- Ayers, W., Quinn, T., & Stovall, D. (2009). *Handbook of Social Justice in Education.* New York: Routledge.
- Grant, C. A., & Chapman, T. (2008). *History of Multicultural Education, Volumes I–VI.* New York: Routledge.
- Ladson-Billings, G. (2009). *The Dreamkeepers: Successful Teachers of African American Children,* 2nd Edition. San Francisco, CA: Jossey-Bass.

I

MOVEMENTS TOWARD ANTI-OPPRESSIVE TEACHER EDUCATION

PREPARING TEACHERS to challenge oppression is not easy. Indeed, anti-oppressive teacher education (i.e., approaches to teacher education that work against oppression) faces significant barriers. Many people in society do not acknowledge that everyday practices in schools often comply with or contribute to racism, sexism, classism, heterosexism, and other forms of oppression. Many people do not agree that change is needed in the oftentimes invisible ways that schools and society favor or privilege certain groups or identities and disadvantage or marginalize others. And those people who do must challenge commonsensical views of what and who schools and teachers are "supposed" to be that draw on historical traditions and cultural myths that make change difficult. Common and commonsensical notions of "real" or "good" teaching do not involve challenging oppression and can actually help to perpetuate rather than change the oppressive status quo of schools and society.

Traditionally, teacher education programs have contributed to this problem by not significantly troubling the ways that dominating views and practices of "good" teachers contribute to oppression and hinder anti-oppressive change. Teacher educators have not always agreed with the public: In recent years in the United States, ballot initiatives and governmental dictates have increasingly attempted to prescribe only certain approaches to teacher education as a way to ensure that "good" teachers are produced, and many teacher educators have protested and resisted such dictates for being oppressive (leading them to be criti-

1

cized for being "out of touch" with the public). But many teacher educators similarly rely on commonsensical ideas of good teaching. Even teacher educators committed to social justice seem to depart little from discourses of teaching that have historically had currency and privilege in U.S. society. And when they do wish to depart from commonsensical discourses, they often confront institutional demands, disciplinary constraints, and social pressures that significantly hinder their ability to bring about change.

Over the course of two years, from 2000 to 2002, I examined eighty elementary and secondary teacher education programs across the United States that made explicit a goal of addressing issues of anti-oppressive education. The programs varied by type of institution (public and private/religious universities and liberal arts colleges). The programs also varied by geographic location (across the United States and in urban, suburban, and remote areas). Although all the programs shared a commitment to anti-oppressive education, they varied in their terminology (using such terms as *social justice, multiculturalism, equity, diversity, feminism, critical*) and the programmatic implementation of this commitment (through course topics, course assignments, program requirements, mission statements, and/or field placements). Initially, my list of possible teacher education programs grew to over two hundred institutions, identified in several ways: my previous knowledge of the programs, the publications and activism of individual faculty members in the programs, referrals by teacher educators familiar with anti-oppressive educational issues, and searches on the Internet. Expecting that programs would be working toward social justice in ways responsive to their unique social and political contexts, I selected a diverse group of programs that represented a broad yet balanced range of practices, types of institutions, sizes, and geographic locations.

For all institutions, I surveyed the most recent materials available (including program descriptions, certification requirements, mission statements, course descriptions, and course syllabi) in print and on the Internet. I focused primarily on the language used to discuss anti-oppressive educational issues and the discourses that framed or were framed by that language. For exactly half of these institutions, I supplemented my analysis of written materials by informally interviewing (in person and over e-mail) faculty and students about their programs' visions and/or practices of anti-oppressive teacher education. These programs were a representative selection, based on type of institution and region. As expected, the programs varied significantly in content and requirements. However, in my search for shared discourses or common movements among them, I did find that the programs discussed, in some form, at least three types of teachers that they aimed to prepare: teachers who are learned practitioners, teachers who are researchers, and teachers who are professionals. In chapter 1, I describe each movement and point to the potential of each one for complicity with various oppressions as well as for anti-oppressive change.

In chapters 2 through 5, I explore alternative discourses on what it could mean to center teacher education on challenging oppression: preparing teachers for crisis, preparing teachers for uncertainty, preparing teachers for healing, and preparing teachers for activism. I do not suggest that the first three discourses should be abandoned, and the alternative ones wholeheartedly adopted, nor do I argue that the various discourses do not, in some ways, overlap. However, I do suggest that we not continue to privilege the first three discourses in teacher education programs and that we instead look critically at the contradictory ways that they help us to work toward social justice. No practice is always anti-oppressive, and teacher education programs have a responsibility to explore the anti-oppressive changes made possible by alternative discourses on teaching.

1

THREE TEACHER IMAGES IN U.S. TEACHER EDUCATION PROGRAMS

THE DIVERSITY AND COMPLEXITY of teacher education programs across the United States make it difficult, if not impossible, to say that *this* is what they are all like. It would be problematic to oversimplify the important work being done in teacher education programs that aim toward social justice, and it would be regrettable to dismiss their work based on such oversimplifications and generalizations. Such are not my goals. Rather, my goals are to examine the popular images of "good teachers" that seem to inform the ways that we are preparing our future teachers, and then to illuminate the hidden ways that these images can hinder our efforts to challenge oppression.

In what follows, I describe three images of "good teachers"—teachers as learned practitioners, teachers as researchers, and teachers as professionals—that emerge across U.S. teacher education programs working toward social justice, and I examine ways that they can hinder anti-oppressive change. Admittedly, I produce portraits of these images that are shared across the programs and thus are quite general and simplistic. I wish to emphasize that I am not suggesting that any teacher education program is intentionally producing teachers that mirror my simplified synthesis, nor am I suggesting that no program goes above and beyond these images as they produce teachers who can work against oppression in multiple, complex, and insightful ways. Rather, I am suggesting that, even in programs doing incredible work, there are insidious ways in which commonsensical ideas of teaching and teachers influence our goals and thus can hinder our movement toward social justice. I acknowledge the discomfort involved in critiquing programs that we have worked hard to create, especially since I have taught in some of the programs that I surveyed. However, I encourage readers to interpret my analysis not as a dismissal of all that we are doing, but rather as an example of the kind of ongoing work we need to do as we continue to find new ways to improve our programs and challenge the status quo.

TEACHER AS LEARNED PRACTITIONER

Sometimes humorously, sometimes not, the materials of some teacher education programs refuted or toyed with the popular refrain that "those who can, do, and those who can't, teach" as a way to recruit talented and high-achieving students into their programs. Such responses were symbolic of a larger movement among the programs to produce knowledgeable, skillful, and learned teachers. The materials of the programs included discussion—sometimes at length—of what students would be learning and why such learning was important. Although cultural myths would have many believe that teachers are self-made and learn how to teach only through experience and not through study, materials were often quite insistent that the programs aimed to teach students to teach in ways that did not merely repeat commonsensical approaches to teaching.

Students needed to learn three main things. First, they needed to learn about young students, especially dominant theories of who they are, how they develop, and how they learn. It seemed to be taken for granted that the more teachers know about how students learn, the more they can raise student achievement, and as has been the case for the past century, this meant learning about psychology: Educational psychology was the field most required by the programs. In fact, courses on "theories of learning" often consisted solely or primarily of psychological theories, implying that they are one and the same. The programs devoted some attention to differences among students, such as racial, class, and gender differences, though differences in language, sexual orientation, and religion were less noticeable.

Second, students needed to learn about what they will teach and to demonstrate this knowledge against the learning standards in their fields of study. Research has sometimes attributed low student achievement to teachers who teach in subject areas where they have not earned an academic major or minor. Perhaps not surprisingly, with some flexibility for nonstandard majors, programs required that students either major in their area of certification or take a certain number and/or distribution of courses in their area, as well as have a certain grade-point average. No program required that students take significant coursework in critical perspectives on their field, such as multicultural critiques of mathematics, feminist histories of the natural sciences, postcolonial perspectives on English literature, and queer re-readings of history, which parallels the requirement that students learn and demonstrate proficiency in the fields as the fields have traditionally been defined.

Third, students needed to learn about how to teach, from classroom management to instruction in the disciplines. The programs showed much variability in teaching how to teach, from the amount of coursework they required in "methods," to the amount of time and the timing of field experiences, to the level of involvement of practicing teachers. This variability is perhaps not surprising, given the extant research on the difficulties teacher education programs face in helping students to challenge their preconceptions and teach in ways that question tradition or common sense and that implement different theories or approaches. This variability is also not surprising, given the emphasis programs placed on the notion that learning how to teach is a complicated process that does not necessarily have one answer. Nonetheless, there were consistencies. Many programs constructed their curricula in a scaffolded way, where there was some sense of progression from foundational knowledge to advanced knowledge. All programs required some blending of theory with practical experience, ranging from observations of others in earlier coursework to reflections on one's own teaching in methods courses. Almost no program made central use of readings and assignments on anti-oppressive methods that focused on differences, equity, power, and oppression.

Wherein lies the problem? It is certainly important that teachers try to know their students, know their subjects, and know how to teach, and programs should continue to ensure that teachers are learned in these ways. However, it is equally important that teachers know the limits of their knowledge. There is much that teachers can never know about their students, such as the students' experiences and desires of which even the students themselves may not be aware, and these excesses can get in the way of addressing students and tailoring lessons to them. Furthermore, even if teachers could fully know their students, the dominant frameworks being used to know students, as with any theory or perspective, are necessarily partial, making only certain insights possible and others, impossible. Psychological models are not the only ways to know our students, and different models or lenses can lead to different insights. It is problematic, then, to privilege only certain (psychological) ways of knowing students.

So, too, with coming to know the disciplines. Learning a subject matter often requires that students learn what some have defined as the official knowledge in the field and think as do experts in the field. For example, there are many ways to think mathematically and many ways to use mathematics, including ways that we have yet to realize. Different ways can lead to different social and political outcomes, as when a way of thinking mathematically privileges certain values or when a way of using math benefits only certain groups in society. Yet, those leading the field of math education have incorporated into the "learning standards" only certain ways of thinking and using. Learning to standards in the disciplines is a practice of repetition, of repeating or perpetuating only certain ways of knowing or doing the disciplines, and since any perspective or practice is partial, learning to standards is a practice that reinforces the privilege of only certain perspectives and groups in society.

This is true even when learning how to teach. What counts as the knowledge and skills that students need to learn to become teachers (as defined by state credentialing agencies or national accrediting organizations) have become privileged because certain people asked certain questions and used certain frameworks to produce the answers. What counts as official knowledge in teacher education cannot help but be partial, regardless of how it is defined and by whom. So, while learning more knowledge and becoming learned practitioners may help to address some oppressions in society, it can help to perpetuate others. This is not to say that teachers and students should not be learning what programs are currently teaching. Rather, it is to say that teachers and students need simultaneously to learn about the limitations and political ramifications of their knowledge.

Fortunately, some teacher educators are working to steer the movement of making teachers learned practitioners in anti-oppressive directions, and their work comes in the form of troubling knowledge. Here I mean troubling in both senses of the word. First, troubling knowledge means to complicate knowledge, to make knowledge problematic. This does not mean to reject knowledge. Rather, it means to work *paradoxically* with knowledge, that is, to simultaneously use knowledge to see what different insights, identities, practices, and changes it makes possible while critically examining that knowledge (and how it came to be known) to see what insights and the like it closes off. When teacher educators ask, What do psychological perspectives tell us about youth and learning?, they also ask, What other knowledge about youth can we learn from gaps in psychology or from theories and methods other than psychological ones? When they ask, What do the disciplines as currently defined and taught tell us about who we are and the world in which we live?, they also ask, What are different ways to learn, use, and critique the disciplines, as well as different ways to think disciplinarily? When they ask, What does educational research tell us about how to teach?, they also ask, What are ways that current educational research makes only certain ways of teaching desirable and doable and thinkable? They tell us that teachers and students need to see knowledge, especially the official knowledge of schools, as political and partial. Particularly regarding the standards for learning, they tell us that students do need to learn toward the standards (since the standards reflect what knowledge and skills are valued in society), but also need to think critically about the partial nature of the standards.

Second, "troubling knowledge" means knowledge that is disruptive, discomforting, and problematizing. In addition to disrupting the knowledge that is being taught or that was already learned, some teacher educators are teaching or constructing knowledge that is itself already disruptive. Too often, the value of knowledge in teacher education stems from its ability to be applied in the classroom and to make our teaching "effective" or "successful." That is, what makes knowledge in teacher education valuable is the comfort or assurance it allows us to feel in our subsequent teaching. Valuable and desirable knowledge is that which makes "good" teaching possible, and recent calls for a "knowledge base" in teacher education often target just this kind of knowledge. In contrast, what is not often desired or valued is knowledge that reveals ways that common views of "good" teaching are neither possible nor desirable, and perhaps more significantly, ways that engaging in what many define as "good" teaching can actually be quite oppressive. It is not often comforting to learn things that make our students or our disciplines or the process of teaching even more difficult to know. Not surprisingly, what teachers often desire learning is a comforting knowledge that helps us to stay blinded to those aspects of teaching that we cannot bear to see, especially aspects that comply with oppression. What is comforting, at least at a subconscious level, is a repetition of familiar, doable, commonsensical practices, not disruption and change.

In response, some teacher educators are teaching about the knowledge that we often resist learning, including the discomforting knowledge about our own complicity with oppression or the aspects of teaching that are neither controllable nor rational. Rather than only teach what is already known, they also teach what we desire not to know (the contradictions, the gaps, the partialities), and then explore their political ramifications, be they oppressive, anti-oppressive, or otherwise. If knowledge is always partial and already has political effects, then becoming a learned practitioner can never be about mastery or full knowledge; the goal can never be to fill that partiality and erase the politics. Furthermore, the goal can never be to learn the "better" body of knowledge, since any body of knowledge is partial. Rather, the goal is to examine the different uses and effects of different bodies of knowledge, and explore the anti-oppressive changes made possible from them. Anti-oppressive teacher education requires that practitioners be "learned" in very different ways.

TEACHER AS RESEARCHER

Without exception, all the teacher education programs suggested that "good" teaching requires that teachers be ongoing learners, especially of teaching. Troubling the distinction between teacher and learner, the programs suggested paradoxically that, on the one hand, teachers needed to become learned before they can teach, while on the other, teachers can never be fully or finally learned. As some programs put it, teachers need to continually learn, to be lifelong learners, to themselves be perpetual students of teaching. This imperative to constantly reflect on one's own teaching and explore new methods applied to both pre-service and inservice teachers.

In preservice teacher education, all programs incorporated some form of self-reflection, such as journals, essays, and seminar discussions about their lesson-planning and classroom experiences. Some programs devoted some time to teaching a particular research methodology for self-study (such as by identifying questions or problems in their own teaching, surveying the research literature, experimenting with different teaching practices, and reflecting on the results and implications). Many programs required student teachers to conduct some form of research project, such as by examining teaching practices that could address the unique needs of the student teachers' immediate classroom context. Such a requirement helped to center teacher education on problems and questions raised in student teachers' field experiences rather than on abstracted concepts of teaching that were dictated and ordered before students even entered the classroom. Such a requirement also worked to bridge the gap between theory (often seen as irrelevant) and practice (often informed by common sense and pre-conceptions). Learning to teach, according to this view, involved reflecting on and raising questions about one's teaching.

The same applied to inservice preparation. Programs that offered educational opportunities for practicing teachers (such as coursework for continuing education, recertification, and master-of-teaching degrees) stressed the development of research skills and opportunities for research. From workshops on research methodology, to courses that required ongoing conversations (such as in journals or essays) between one's experiences and relevant research literature, to invitations to participate in collaborative research projects with university instructors and researchers, the programs often stressed the importance of teachers becoming researchers as a way to continue developing professionally and improving their teaching.

Wherein lies the problem? Doing research does not itself necessarily promise anti-oppressive change. I am not suggesting that teachers should not learn research skills, since challenging the status quo requires learning new ways to assess one's own teaching and finding new alternatives. However, teachers should not be learning to do research only as we have traditionally conceptualized research. As with other forms of research, teacher research can both comply with and challenge different forms of oppression. It is entirely possible, for example, for teachers to research *topics* that do not address issues of social justice (or even to ask questions that themselves perpetuate stereotypes), define the *goals* of research in problematic ways, use *methods* that perpetuate harmful social relationships, and present and use the *results* of the research in ways that comply with or contribute to different forms of oppression.

For example, consider the topics of research. Some teachers and teacher educators seem to believe that learning to teach toward social justice requires that they first learn the "basics," such as how to manage a classroom and how to teach their disciplines, and afterward, incorporate or add anti-oppressive methods. Such a view presupposes that the basics of teaching are somehow neutral practices unimplicated in the dynamics of oppression and ignores research that reveals ways in which teaching practices are always and already implicated in oppression. Learning the basics of teaching does not precede learning about oppression in teaching, and therefore, teacher research that does not interrupt the oppressions already in play may reinforce the very practices that are problematic.

Some teacher education programs did incorporate teacher research on anti-oppressive topics, such as when teaching a form of "action research" that involved social critique. Even in action research, however, the goals can be problematic if they are not counterintuitive. Thus, as some of these teacher educators pointed out, when learning to teach, teachers should not be trying to gain more and more knowledge and come closer and closer to being fully learned or to acquiring a repertoire of proven methods that "work." Teachers should not be merely acquiring more knowledge about who is in the classroom, what they have yet to learn, and what works for them. Such questions are important, but by assuming that the problem is a lack of knowledge on the part of teachers, they fail to address ways in which both our teaching and our research often consist of a desire to repeat oppressive practices (because, as argued earlier, they provide some sense of comfort). Some teacher educators suggested that, along with examining what we have yet to learn, it is important to examine what we have already learned (and desire continuing to learn) and simultaneously what we desire not learning: Who do we desire in our classrooms, what do our students desire learning, how do we desire teaching, and how do these desires make anti-oppressive changes difficult? Teacher research needs to examine teachers' desires for only certain things and resistances to others.

It is also important that teachers conduct and use research in anti-oppressive ways. Some teacher educators emphasized that, even if the topic of study is social justice, it is certainly possible to collect data in commonsensical, modernist ways; to analyze the data against research and theory that do not themselves address issues of social justice; and to represent the findings in conventional ways. Some methods of research can also perpetuate oppressive (patriarchal, racist) social relationships between teachers and students, depending on how the data are collected and analyzed. Thus, some teacher educators suggested that, as an alternative, teachers need to learn to *collect* data in ways that work against power differentials between participants and in ways that aim to make anti-oppressive changes in the research context, such as when drawing on aspects of feminist, activist, and collaborative research methodologies. Teachers need to learn to *analyze* the data using theoretical frameworks that focus on issues of social justice. And teachers need to learn to *re-present* and discuss their findings in ways that invite the reader to ask troubling questions about what is being reported. Anti-oppressive methods do not aim to know what is really there in the classroom and then to communicate and/or apply this knowledge as proven practices for teaching. Rather, they aim to explore how different implications and uses are made possible by studying what is there in different ways. There is not a best practice for teaching, just as there is not a best method for doing research. Any practice or method is necessarily partial.

Anti-oppressive research is not unlike anti-oppressive teaching. Both are paradoxical (where teachers both make use of and problematize something), and both are partial, in both senses of the word. Like teaching, which can never lead to being fully learned, research is never *complete*, which means the researcher needs to continue researching even while troubling what was just concluded. And like teaching, which can never be without gaps and perspective, research is never *neutral*, which means the researcher needs to explore alternatives to even the anti-oppressive perspectives under investigation. It is easy to imagine teacher research that makes little or no use of anti-oppressive topics, goals, and methods. But as some programs demonstrate, it is possible to train teacher researchers to strive to make constant use of such things. Teachers can learn to constantly ask, What are hidden ways that my practices reinforce oppression? What new theories can I use to make sense of my experiences in different ways, and how do these new interpretations lead to different political implications? What alternative practices are made possible when I "do" research on my teaching in noncommonsensical ways? What are ways to "do" research in my classroom that themselves can bring about anti-oppressive change? What are ways to talk about my research that can prompt the reader to problematize my analyses?

Learning to teach in anti-oppressive ways does not simply involve acquiring more knowledge about what is out there or about how things work in the world or in the classroom. And continuing to learn to teach does not simply involve getting closer to the state of fully knowing what it means to teach well. Learning to teach in anti-oppressive ways also needs to involve examining how "good" teaching can be problematic.

TEACHER AS PROFESSIONAL

All of the teacher education programs met state requirements for the certification of teachers. In other words, all were accredited by some educational entity, including state departments of education and the

National Council for Accreditation of Teacher Education, to prepare students to teach in public elementary, middle, and/or secondary schools. Although it is imaginable that a program might discuss certification requirements as hurdles imposed from above, or unpleasant but necessary steps, or mere rules of the game, no program did that. Rather, the programs discussed certification requirements as beginning and even praiseworthy stages in professional development. Learning to teach was characterized as an entry into a profession, and a noble one at that.

This common discourse of professionalism reflects a national movement to professionalize teaching. Some teacher advocates argue that, by defining teaching as a profession, larger numbers of talented students might be attracted to teaching instead of to other, more socially prestigious professions. Most significant for my analysis, some advocates argue that doing more to treat teaching as a profession (that is, making the teaching profession more like other professions) could improve the quality of education, and that the way to do this is by requiring that teachers and the institutions preparing them meet certain standards. Some programs made it clear how they met accreditation standards by highlighting some of the standards and describing the relevant components of their program. Some programs made it clear that their graduates met and exceeded certification standards by showcasing sample student achievements. And some programs with continuing or graduate education for practicing teachers made it clear that they helped experienced teachers advance in their careers by offering courses or components of courses on mentoring, researching, and other skills that "master" teachers would need.

As I already discussed earlier in this chapter, it is problematic for some in society to prescribe ahead of time what all teachers need to know and do and be in order to be "good" teachers, or even to be allowed to teach. Standards can be problematic, especially when they insist on the repetition of only certain knowledge and do not encourage troubling knowledge and looking beyond. By critiquing the standardization of teaching, I am certainly not advocating that anyone be allowed to teach anything in any way—such freedom could mean that teachers now have license to teach in overtly oppressive ways. Nor am I advocating doing away with all standards—the standards can often be a helpful list to which teachers can point and say, Here are the knowledge, skills, and perspectives that are valued in society and that, to succeed in this society, you need to learn. Rather, I am emphasizing the need to problematize any effort to predetermine what it means to be a "good" teacher. Commonsensical definitions of good teaching are often complicit with different forms of oppression. So, too, are more "progressive" definitions of good teaching since even practices of anti-oppressive teaching are partial and contradictory, are momentary and situated, and thus, are always in need of being rethought. It is never possible to say that a given practice is always and fully and unproblematically anti-oppressive. The standards of anti-oppressive teaching (if such a phrase can be used) are always in need of themselves being problematized.

Some teacher educators suggested that it was not possible to say that a teacher is always or fully or unproblematically anti-oppressive. An anti-oppressive teacher is not something that someone is. Rather, it is something that someone is always becoming. There are at least two reasons why. First, as is the case with standards of anti-oppressive teaching, the actual *practice* of anti-oppressive teaching is always in need of being problematized. No practice, in and of itself, is anti-oppressive. A practice can be anti-oppressive in one situation and quite oppressive in another. Or it can be simultaneously oppressive in one way and anti-oppressive in another. So, too, with the practitioner. A teacher can be teaching anti-oppressively in one situation, but from situation to situation, different oppressions play out differently and new responses must be envisioned and engaged. The anti-oppressive teacher, then, is akin to an ideal. It is something we strive for and transitionally become in our practices but never fully are. And the moment we say that we are, the moment that we fix our identities and begin repeating only certain practices and knowledge and relations that we believe are anti-oppressive, we stop doing the necessary work of problematizing how any approach to teaching is partial. We cannot help but teach in problematic ways if we feel comfortable with the notion that we exemplify the anti-oppressive teacher.

Second, commonsensical notions of what it means to be a teacher do not often center on anti-oppressive roles and responsibilities. Teaching in anti-oppressive ways often contradicts what we think it means to teach, causing the identity of "teacher" to conflict sharply with some anti-oppressive teaching practices. As a result, teachers may question whether they are really teaching, students may question their authority as teachers, and observers may question their competence and accomplishments since the teachers are not doing what they are "supposed" to be doing. The identity of "anti-oppressive teacher" is paradoxical, which means that an anti-oppressive teacher is always trying to change what it means to be a teacher. The teacher is always becoming anti-oppressive but never fully is.

Why is this important? By saying that teachers are professionals, we fix the identity of "teacher." The professionalized identity of teacher is just as normative as the cultural myths of teacher. Both say who teachers are supposed to be, and neither requires that teachers teach in anti-oppressive ways. It is entirely possible for a professional to be complicit with oppression, to make no effort to address oppression, and for that matter, to insist that teaching be done in traditional, commonsensical, and oppressive ways. Many professionals in U.S. society, after all, use their professions to advance socially oppressive causes, as with medical doctors who pathologize certain desires or lawyers who prosecute certain acts. Professions themselves are not necessarily oppressive, nor are they necessarily anti-oppressive, which means that professionalizing teaching can lead to some anti-oppressive changes but can also close off other changes. I am not saying that teachers are not professionals, nor am I saying that teaching should not be a profession. I am saying, however, that we need to trouble the commonsensical notion that increasing the professionalization of teaching will help to address oppressions in schools and society. After all, there are many ways to define the group "teachers," and different definitions can lead to different changes.

In the next four chapters, I explore four alternative ways to define teachers, drawing on a range of perspectives, experiences, and concepts not often used in educational research. These alternatives are not the "best" ways to prepare anti-oppressive educators, nor are they without limitations. They do, however, suggest approaches to preparing teachers that can make possible new movements toward social justice. And fortunately, they are approaches that some teacher educators have already begun using, examining, and broadening.

QUESTIONS FOR REFLECTION AND DISCUSSION

1. (Comprehension) What are similarities and differences between the notions of "troubling knowledge" and "always becoming?"
2. (Comprehension) What are the three dominant images of "good teachers" in teacher-education programs, and how does each image both advance and hinder social justice in education?
3. (Concretization) How does the teacher-education program in which you were/are teaching and learning reflect and challenge these dominant images in its policies, practices, curriculum, and culture?
4. (Critique) What are alternative images of "good teachers" or "good teaching" in educational institutions as well as in popular culture, and how does each image both enable and hinder anti-oppressive education?

SAMPLING OF NEW RESOURCES

For analyses of dominant images in schools and society of teachers and who should teach:

*   Blount, J. M. (2005). *Fit to Teach: Same-Sex Desire, Gender, and School Work in the Twentieth Century.* Albany, NY: State University of New York Press.
*   Britzman, D. (2003). *Practice Makes Practice: A Critical Study of Learning to Teach,* Revised Edition. Albany, NY: State University of New York Press.
*   Cochran-Smith, M., & Zeichner, K. (2008). *Handbook of Research on Teacher Education,* 3rd Edition. New York: Routledge.
*   Meiners, E. (2006). *Right to Be Hostile: Schools, Prisons, and the Making of Public Enemies.* New York: Routledge.

2

PREPARING TEACHERS FOR CRISIS:
A SAMPLE LESSON

WHAT IT MEANS TO BE A STUDENT

WHILE I WAS IN COLLEGE, I taught at a summer daycare program for preschool and elementary school students. My primary placement was in the afternoon class for the older students, although I often taught a morning class for the preschoolers as well. With the preschoolers, I tried to blend activities with goals that ranged from "getting along" and increasing self-awareness, to expressing oneself through arts and crafts, to learning basic academic concepts in preparation for the upcoming kindergarten year. Memories of one of my students, M, still move me.

M was quite a handful, and one of the other preschool teachers would often laugh in sympathy when I would share stories of the day's events. M did not follow instructions well. Sometimes I led an art activity and M would insist on playing with toys or, when joining the activity, would create only what M wanted to create. Sometimes we went on field trips, and M would have difficulty listening quietly to the speaker at the museum or following the rules at the hands-on science exhibit. M was restless if required to sit for too long and rowdy if required to sit quietly for too long, and often spoke loudly, especially when unwilling to take turns speaking. During one particular recess, M did not feel like playing with the other students and chose instead to hang out at the edge of the playground, near a short palm tree. Within moments, M went from lounging near the tree to swinging on a branch to breaking off the branch and wielding it as a sword.

For some reason, upon seeing that sword-branch, I quickly lost my temper and started yelling so loudly that my throat became hoarse. I made the entire class sit quietly and take a "time out," mainly because I needed to take my own time out. I was a teacher who wanted to have control over the classroom. For me, M's behavior was a sign that I was not being an effective teacher, that I was not reaching M, and therefore that M was not learning and becoming the kind of student that I desired. I remember leaving school that day feeling exhausted and slightly embarrassed when I ran into the teacher whose classroom was nearest the playground. She did not mention my outburst, but she did say that it sounded as though I had had a hard day. No kidding. When I said that I felt as though I still had a lot to learn about teaching, she suggested that I think about why I became so upset. What was I expecting from M, and what was M telling me in return?

I realized that M became a different kind of student during less structured class time. When not required to conform to an art lesson, M would hunch over with crayons in hand, deep in concentration, to produce a piece of art to give to me. When not required to listen passively to a lecture, M would pull me aside and ask me questions about the museum exhibit. M's varied behaviors were indirectly communicating something about what it did and did not mean for M to learn. It was not that M was trying to be bad or could not distinguish bad from good. It was not that M did not want to learn or was unable to learn. Rather, there was something about what it meant to learn in a traditional classroom that did not work for M, and M's way of communicating that mismatch played out as "misbehavior." And indeed, rare was the day that M did not have at least one time out. It almost seemed as if the student that the school and I wanted M to be was not a student that M could be.

The morning classes always ended with time for a nap, and knowing M's own tendencies to get into trouble, M often chose to lay a sleeping bag in a corner away from others. Naptime marked the end of the morning class with me and the beginning of the afternoon class with another teacher. More and more frequently, as I would turn down the lights and prepare to leave, M would call me over, and in a whisper, so that the other students would not hear, ask:

"Are you going now?"

"Yes. Are you ready for your nap?"

M's head would nod. "Was I bad today?"

"M, you are not bad. It's just your behavior that sometimes needs to be better."

"I'll be better tomorrow," M would say apologetically. And each time we had this conversation, I would leave with a sense of profound sadness that something was not right.

Over the next several years, many more students like M would enter my classrooms, students who were unable or unwilling to be the kind of student that schools and society often tell them to be. I remember consistently feeling quite frustrated by such students, not only because I assumed that being a student required behaving and thinking in only certain ways, but also because I felt pressure from schools and society to produce this type of student. I once taught middle and high school English classes at a school that clearly prescribed what students were to learn and how they were to demonstrate what it was they learned. Each quarter I was told what books students needed to read, how many and what types of essays they needed to write, what vocabulary words they needed to memorize, and for the final exam, what themes from the books they needed to understand and be able to develop in short essays. Exams were standardized across the department, and grades were to be distributed on a bell curve. In this school, learning meant completing certain assignments and repeating on exams the correct definitions or themes or analyses in a strong essay format, and the closer a student got to saying the right things in the right ways, the higher that student's grade would be.

Of the students who resisted the school's and my attempts to predetermine what they were supposed to learn, the most vocal was N. N often carried a novel from the library to read in spare moments but did not take interest in the books read in class. N quite often asked if I actually thought that what we were reading was interesting, or whether I was teaching it just because I had to. Sometimes N read class materials but would become frustrated in discussions of the themes or the plots or the character development. N wanted to discuss different ways of making sense of the book and would get frustrated with the notion that some ways of interpreting the book were more correct than others and that those correct ways were the ones that mattered on the standardized exams. In contrast, when students were once allowed to write a short story on whatever topic and in whatever format they preferred, N spoke quite excitedly about possible ideas whenever we met in the halls and especially in the computer room while in the midst of writing. In an unusually prompt fashion, N turned in a story that was quite complex, long, and lucid, which surprised me as I had thought that N did not like to write. In contrast to N's short story, N's essays seemed like last-minute efforts: They were often short and riddled with careless errors and undeveloped ideas.

Once, I devoted an entire class period to discussing one particularly significant moment in a novel we were reading. Having posed the overarching question that I wanted us to discuss, I proceeded to ask a range of prodding questions, wrote ideas they brainstormed on the board, and drew a diagram that their responses seemed to suggest. Toward the end of the period, they arrived at what I thought to be an insightful analysis. I pointed to the level of detail and complexity in their notes and discussion, and shared with them my feelings of excitement and pride in their work. Most students continued taking notes, but I saw N staring forward, sitting still for a moment, then hunching forward:

"Why didn't you just tell us the answer in the beginning? Did we have to have this whole discussion?"

"I didn't want to just *tell* you the answer. You don't learn when you're just told an answer. You learn when you figure things out yourself and come to your own answers."

"But you already had the answer. Weren't we just trying to figure out *your* answer?" With raised brows, N smiled slightly at me before continuing to take notes. N had earlier admitted to me that other teachers did not allow students to voice criticisms of their teaching, which is perhaps why N seemed to like coming to my class. My class may have been no different than other classes in requiring that students learn in only certain ways, but at least in my class N could raise concerns about what it meant to learn.

By sharing these stories of M and N, I am not suggesting that a better approach to teaching would have been to let them behave or analyze literature or produce writing in whichever ways they pleased. Mainstream society often places value on certain kinds of behaviors, knowledge, and skills, and schools would disadvantage students by not teaching what often matters in schools and society. I am also not merely suggesting that a better approach to teaching would have been to learn about the particular learning style of individual students and then to tailor the lessons to those differences. Although I do believe that addressing the unique learning styles, needs, and desires of students is important, I also believe that the experiences of M and N point to a problem that lies deeper than our inabilities to create tailored, responsive, or engaging lessons. After all, if the lesson itself is problematic, then there is little reason to want students engaged. What I am suggesting is that there is something about the very ways we think about learning that can be oppressive.

Later in this book, I will argue that oppression can result from what students learn as well as from how students learn. But here, I want to argue that oppression can also result from who we allow students to be. There is something oppressive about what we often say it means to be a student and, simultaneously, what it means to learn.

WHAT IT MEANS TO LEARN

I once began a semester-long course for student teachers by explaining my belief that I, like other teachers, often define educational goals for myself and my students in ways that have been significantly shaped by the messages and images permeating society about what it means to learn. Turning to the chalkboard, I drew two diagrams to illustrate the view of learning that I have confronted most often (Figure 1).

The top diagram illustrated a student who was not learning. The student entered school in September with little knowledge and few skills in the mind (as reflected in the empty glass). Because the school did not know what and/or how to teach, or because the student was unable or unwilling to do the work necessary to learn, the student left school in June without having acquired much new knowledge and skills, thus feeling frustrated and unhappy.

Learning from "Bad" Teaching

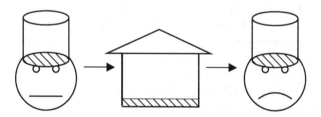

Learning from "Good" Teaching

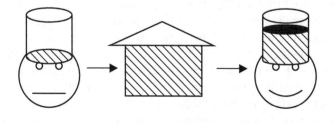

Fig. 1

In contrast is the student in the bottom diagram. Like the student in the top diagram, this one entered school in September with little knowledge and skills. However, the school was filled with knowledge of subject matter as well as teaching strategies that enabled the student to acquire new knowledge and skills. The result was a student satisfied with having learned something new, or at least with having learned what the school was supposed to have taught. According to this view, educated students were those who ended the school year with more than they began, and effective teachers were those who helped fill students' minds. Learning was about learning *more*. "Expanding" our minds. "Building" a foundation of knowledge and skills. "Increasing" our understanding of the world. Such a view has become taken-for-granted in discussions of the goals of education, so much so that teachers and researchers looking to improve teaching often search for the strategies that can get students from empty glasses to full ones. Sometimes the person filling the glass is the teacher (through lectures or guided discussions), and sometimes it is the student (through discovery or collaborative inquiry), but the goal remains the same: to fill that glass.

These diagrams were quite simplistic, but I explained that they did seem to reflect ways that many people, including I, thought of teaching and learning. I often did have clear ideas of the concepts and skills and dispositions that I hoped students would learn as they engaged in the activities and completed the assignments that I laid out in our syllabi. In fact, I wondered aloud, Was this not the view of learning upon which "learning standards" were based, namely, that we identify what knowledge and skills we want students to learn, and afterward we assess whether or not students can demonstrate that they indeed learned such things? Furthermore, was this not the view of effective teaching upon which current proposals to reform schools were based, namely, that we reward those schools that can get their students to demonstrate such learning and punish those who do not?

Turning back to the chalkboard, I then drew an alternative view of learning (Figure 2). The top diagram offered a different interpretation of the commonsensical view of learning that was captured in Figure 1, and suggested that such a view actually hindered movements toward social justice. There were several reasons why. The student could not have entered school as a blank slate. The student entered school filled with knowledge that the student already learned from the family, the community, the media, and life experiences, including prior schooling. The student might have learned that people who lived "over there" were dirty and people who looked "like that" could not be trusted, or that some activities were appropriate for girls and others were appro-

Learning in Comforting Ways

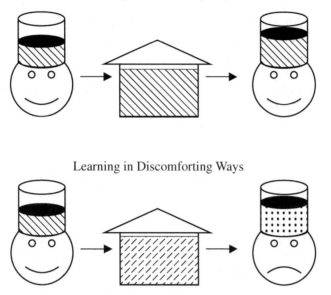

Learning in Discomforting Ways

Fig. 2

priate for boys, or that certain beliefs, values, and feelings were proper or natural. Of course, not everything that the student already learned was problematic, but much of this knowledge had been culled together from the cultural myths, stereotypes, and taken-for-granted assumptions that permeated daily life. In particular, much of what the student already learned consisted of the ideas that have, thus far, helped the student to make sense of who the student was and to navigate the world in which the student lived, including ideas of what was normal or good, or what it meant to be happy or to belong. The student already learned things that helped the student to feel comfortable with what got repeated in daily life, and thus, already learned to feel comfortable with uncritical assumptions that supported the status quo.

Some of my students responded that I seemed to be oversimplifying the first model. Don't many teachers acknowledge that students enter school with much misinformation about the world and thus define learning not only as adding what students do not yet know but also as correcting what students already know? Students who never knew how to spell "chew" would add that word to their vocabulary, while students who mistakenly thought the spelling to be "choo" would replace the wrong spelling with the right one. Students who never knew where babies come from would add an understanding of sexual reproduction to their knowledge of life sciences, while students who mistakenly believed the cartoons about storks would replace the wrong information with the correct one. I admitted that I had not made this connection and agreed that this was certainly a limitation of my diagrams. However, I suggested that the notion of "correcting" what students know did seem to lead to the same end result, namely, that students acquire what some in society determined ahead of time to be the things that they were supposed to learn. When teachers correct what students already know, it seems that they are still hoping to fill that glass with only certain things.

Perhaps more important, the notion that teachers can correct what students already know does not often account for the unpredictable ways that students' prior knowledge can invite and/or hinder new learning. What students already know when entering school functions as filters or backdrops or lenses for what they experience, process, make sense of, act on, and otherwise learn in school. For example, a student might have understood a lesson or part of a lesson on nutrition because the lesson paralleled what the student's parent taught earlier on. A student might have dismissed a lesson on racial discrimination because it did not parallel what the student observed on television or in the neighborhood. A student might have felt bored during a lesson on a particular poem because the student already studied the poem last year and did not feel there was anything new to learn. A student might have felt excited by a lesson on a particular law of physics because, for months, the student had unsuccessfully tried to get a science exhibit to work. What and how students learn is influenced by a desire to relearn only certain things, especially only certain ways of making sense of the world, as well as by a resistance to learning other things, especially things that reveal the problematic nature of prior knowledge.

I suggested that these oftentimes subconscious feelings of desire and resistance are central to the process of learning. They should not be viewed as hindrances to learning, and thus, be repressed or ignored or overpowered. Rather, they should become part of the very things that students study. Students' desires for and resistances to learning need to become part of what they are learning.

Some of my students responded that I now seemed to be going in the opposite direction. Rather than oversimplifying one model, I seemed to be making another model unnecessarily complicated. Why require that students examine their own emotions and dispositions? What is significant about learning that we have these desires and resistances? Why not simply require that students learn the more correct ways of thinking about the world: This is why differences are valuable, how stereotypes are harmful, what people are really like, and where oppression plays out invisibly. It may be true that the standards (put forth by national educational organizations) that currently define what all students are supposed to learn contain very little that explicitly addresses oppression, thereby reinforcing the commonsensical idea that academic knowledge and skills have little to do with oppression. As it stands, the insistence on "meeting standards" is an insistence on complying with what some in society have defined as common sense. However, can't we simply change the standards so that students are required to learn about the different ways that oppression plays out in society and in the various disciplines, and ways to challenge oppression?

I agreed that such changes would be heartening. However, I suggested that they would still need to be written in a way that refuses to say that they are *the end goals* of learning. Why? I suggested that any way of making sense of the world is necessarily partial: Only certain people with certain values and experiences have made certain choices to create these perspectives. Any perspective has strengths and weaknesses and can make possible only certain insights and social changes. This applies even to my own perspectives. Although my perspective may more explicitly address social injustices, it would be irresponsible to say, This way of making sense of the world is problem-free. Thus, written into the standards would need to be a requirement that students look beyond the standards to examine its partial and problematic nature, especially regarding issues of oppression. The new standards cannot simply replace one partial view of the world with another, even if it does do more to raise awareness of oppression.

Perhaps more important, challenging oppression requires more than raising awareness about more progressive perspectives on the world. The reason we fail to do more to challenge oppression is not merely that we do not know enough about oppression, but also that we often do not *want* to know more about oppression. It is not our lack of knowledge but our resistance to knowledge and our desire for ignorance that often prevent us from changing the oppressive status quo. As noted earlier, we often find comfort in commonsensical ideas that make sense of the status quo, just as we often feel uncomfortable with ideas that disrupt norms. So, although it would be important to incorporate into the standards more knowledge of oppression and skills to challenge oppression, it would also be important to address the political, social, *emotional* reasons why oppression so often plays out invisibly and unchallenged in our lives. Students need to ask: Why do I often feel invested in relearning only certain things? What effect does relearning only certain things have on my sense of self, my relations with others, my belonging in this world? And similarly, why do schools and society seem invested in my learning only certain things? What effect does teaching only certain things have on race relations, socioeconomic distinctions, gender norms, and so forth? What's up with this investment?

What is significant here is the recognition that challenging oppression does not consist solely of changing the ways that individuals think and feel. Challenging oppression requires addressing the broader social context in which we live. After all, the taken-for-granted views of the world that individuals carry often reflect the commonsensical ideas that permeate mainstream society. Our views do not arise from nowhere. Similarly, the investment that individuals place in certain norms reflects the investment that cultural groups and social institutions place in certain norms or traditions, including norms regarding how different genders should behave, how different races should be categorized, and how different sexual orientations should be valued. The models of learning that I drew on the chalkboard may focus on experiences of the individual student in a single classroom, but they in no way operate separately from the broader dynamics of society. We should not be surprised, then, when the things that students learn in schools do not do much to problematize what they already learned to be common sense. Whether in or out of schools, students were and are learning things that reinforce an oppressive status quo.

This brought me to the bottom diagram in Figure 2 and an anti-oppressive model of learning. As in the top diagram, the student in the bottom diagram entered school with a mind that already contained knowledge and with a desire to affirm and relearn more of the same sort of knowledge. However, the school that the student entered did not seek simply to add to what the student knew and produce a student proficient in the knowledge and skills that some in society have said all students should learn. Rather, the school aimed to challenge the partial nature of both the student's and the school's knowledge. The result was not a student who learned the right things, but a student who both learned what mattered in school and society and unlearned or critically examined what was being learned, how it was being learned, and why it was being learned. Learning involved ending up with knowledge and skills that could not have been predicted by either the student or the teacher.

Some distinctions needed to be made. The student was not learning to ask questions about and critique what was being learned in just any way, nor was the student learning to dismiss the knowledge that had come to matter in society; rather, the student was learning to ask questions about the varied *political implications* of what was being learned (how it both contributed to and challenged oppression). The student was not learning that my progressive view was the better view or that all views and practices were equally valid or equally oppressive; rather, the student was learning that views and practices had different implications in different situations, and that determining an anti-oppressive course of action required assessing these differences. The student was not learning *about* issues of oppression alongside topics from various disciplines; rather, the student was learning to unearth the oppressive tendencies and anti-oppressive possibilities *inherent in* the very ways that we taught the disciplines (whether or not we consciously addressed issues of oppression). Finally, the student was not learning something that brought comfort and closure; rather, the student was learning something that brought discomfort and a desire to do more work.

The frowning face at the end of the diagram generated strong disagreement among my students, several of whom expressed deep concern over the notion that discomfort should be a goal of education. Such a process has never been how U.S. society traditionally thinks about learning.

LEARNING THROUGH CRISIS

That learning might be an uncomfortable process is perhaps a counterintuitive and even disturbing thought, especially if we believe that for learning to occur our schools need to be safe and supportive environments. However, it is not hard to find examples of moments in our everyday teaching when students feel some emotional discomfort while learning something new. Students who believe that "chew" is spelled "choo" might feel some discomfort when realizing that their method for spelling words according to how they sound does not always work. Students who believe that adding numbers is the same as sequencing them (as by believing that $1 + 1 = 2, 2 + 2 = 3, 3 + 3 = 4$, and so forth) might feel upset when realizing that their method for making sense of numbers does not always work. Learning that the ways we have come to make sense of the world does not always work can be disorienting, which helps to explain the signs of frustration, confusion, and anxiety among so many of our students.

Taking this further, when we learn that our ways of making sense of the world are not only inaccurate, but also complicit with different forms of oppression, these feelings of discomfort can intensify. I can remember feeling quite ignorant when I thought I had understood the "themes" or significance of a novel, only to learn that my understanding failed to incorporate ways that racism played out invisibly in the story, just as it does in mainstream society. I can remember feeling quite hypocritical when I thought I was applying a scientific concept in a way that addressed social or environmental ills, only to learn that my application failed to question ways that the concept itself perpetuated gender inequities. I can remember feeling quite overwhelmed when I thought I was a person who was aware of oppression in schools and worked to challenge oppression, only to learn that my understanding of oppression was contradictory, as were my efforts to challenge oppression. Learning things that reveal the partial and oppressive aspects of our knowledge of and actions in the world can lead us into *crisis*.

By "crisis," I mean a state of emotional discomfort and disorientation that calls on students to make some change. When in crisis, students feel that they have just learned something that requires some response. Sometimes this crisis is visceral and noticeable, as when students express feelings of guilt or anger, or in some way resist continuing with the lesson. At other times, this crisis is subdued and subconscious, as when students feel discomfort but are unable to name that feeling. In either case, students who are in crisis are on the verge of some shift and require the opportunity to work through their emotions and disorientation.

What is important, here, is the notion that, while crisis may be a necessary part of the learning process, it is not itself what constitutes learning. Entering crisis is merely the stage where students confront troubling knowledge. To change their thinking in ways that work against oppression, students need a learning process that helps them to *work through* their crisis. Entering crisis can be a condition that makes learning possible, but it can also be a condition that makes learning difficult. For example, I might enter a state of crisis when I realize that my own privileges as, say, a male in society have blinded me to ways that my attempts to challenge racism have unintentionally reinforced biases against women. Although it is possible for my feelings of discomfort to lead me to want to address and challenge my own male privileges, it is also possible, and perhaps more likely, for my feelings to lead me to conclude that challenging multiple forms of oppression simultaneously is impossible, or at least that I am already doing the best that I can. Similarly, students might enter a state of crisis, at least subconsciously, when learning about ways that sexual orientation is socially constructed (that is, ways that people understand and experience sexual orientation differently in different contexts). Although this crisis might lead some students to change the ways they think about sexual difference and even about their own sexual orientation, it might drive others into a state of denial in which they refuse to acknowledge even the possibility that such knowledge can be true. Crisis can lead a student to desire change, but it can also lead a student to resist change even more strongly than before.

When students are in a state of crisis, teachers need to structure experiences that can help students to work through it. Teachers might ask, When students confront discomforting information, what activities, conversations, readings, or experiences can help them to bear being uncomfortable for a while? What experiences can invite them to explore the possibility of making sense of the world and of themselves in very different ways, especially ways that move toward social justice? Planning for such experiences is not easy. Different students experience crisis differently. What leads one student into crisis may not lead another into crisis. Even when students enter crisis simultaneously, their experience of crisis may differ. And what may help one student to work through crisis may not similarly help another. Learning through crisis is not a process that can be standardized for all students. Teachers need to be flexible, attentive to the particularities of different students, and aware of the unpredictability of their responses. The chapters in Part II suggest examples of how to do this in different disciplines.

It is important to reiterate that students are constantly entering crises in schools. These crises may be to different degrees and in different contexts, but they can all offer opportunities to teach against oppression. Albeit unintentionally, teachers are constantly structuring experiences when students enter crises and when students work through crises, but rather than exploring ways that crises can be helpful in challenging oppression, they often try to rid their teaching of crises. Some teachers try to prevent or gloss over uncomfortable moments in order to keep the learning process moving, as when avoiding discussions of "controversial" issues like racism, homophobia, and social differences that can generate heated disagreement and resistance. Some teachers assert that students should not be learning about such emotional and political issues (as if such issues could be separated from the academic disciplines). Some teachers even assert that forcing students to confront such issues and actually trying to induce states of crises are unethical ways of teaching. But what is the alternative?

If students are not experiencing crisis, they likely are not learning things that challenge the knowledge they have already learned that supports the status quo, which means that they likely are not learning to recognize and challenge the oppression that plays out daily in their lives. What is unethical is an approach to teaching and learning that does not involve crisis. Learning is not a comforting process that merely repeats or affirms what students have already learned. Learning is a disarming process that allows students to escape the uncritical, complacent repetition of their prior knowledge and actions. Learning is a disorienting process that raises questions about what was already learned and what has yet to be learned. Learning involves *looking beyond* what students already know, what teachers already know, and what we both are only now coming to know, not by rejecting such knowledge, but by treating it paradoxically, that is, by learning what matters in society (and how it informs my identity, relationships, and actions), while asking why it matters (and how it can reinforce and challenge an oppressive status quo). Such a process cannot help but to be uncomfortable.

There are many forms of crisis that can be quite unproductive for learning, especially if teachers have not structured experiences in which students can work through those crises in useful, meaningful ways. My point, then, is that teachers need to think strategically about the kinds of crises that might be useful for anti-oppressive education and the kinds of experiences that might help students to work through them.

Perhaps the word "crisis" is unnecessarily controversial. In some situations, it can refer to any of a number of things, including quite oppressive experiences. For some people, the word "crisis" seems to suggest a state that is more traumatic than the discomfort involved in the little crises I mentioned earlier, such as when learning about "chew." However, maybe these feelings of discomfort surrounding the word "crisis" are what help to make the term so useful. Maybe we need to start feeling very uncomfortable about the processes of teaching and learning.

QUESTIONS FOR REFLECTION AND DISCUSSION

1. (Comprehension) What does it mean to "learn through crisis," and how is this model of education both similar to and different from the other models presented?
2. (Comprehension) What are educational policies or practices that illustrate each of the various models of education, including policies or practices that you experienced as a student or teacher (such as experiences of learning "more," of discomfort, of resistance)?
3. (Concretization) If you were to design two lessons on the same topic—one lesson that supported students in entering and "working through" crisis, and another lesson that did not—how would the two lessons differ in terms of content and outcome?
4. (Critique) What are limitations of the model of learning through crisis, and how would you visually illustrate an alternative model to address these limitations?

SAMPLING OF NEW RESOURCES

For analyses of teachers, student teachers, and teacher educators who confront discomfort and conflict in the process of addressing diversity and injustice:

- Darling-Hammond, L., French, J., & Paloma Garcia, S. (2005). *Learning to Teach for Social Justice.* New York: Teachers College Press.
- Kumashiro, K. K., & Ngo, B. C. (Eds.). (2006). *Six Lenses for Anti-Oppressive Education: Partial Stories, Improbable Conversations.* New York: Peter Lang.
- North, C. E. (2009). *Teaching for Social Justice?: Voices from the Front Lines.* Boulder, CO: Paradigm Publishers.
- Schulte, A. K. (2009). *Seeking Integrity in Teacher Education: Transforming My Student Teachers, Transforming Myself.* New York: Springer Publishing.
- Social Justice Consortium, & Soohoo, S. (2004). *Essays on Urban Education: Critical Consciousness, Collaboration and the Self.* Cresskill, NJ: Hampton Press.

3

PREPARING TEACHERS FOR UNCERTAINTY:
A SAMPLE LESSON

WHEN I FIRST STARTED WORKING in teacher education programs, I was struck by the large number of student teachers whose understanding of oppression consisted solely of interpersonal interactions that were visibly harmful. To them, it was possible to keep oppression outside of their classrooms by enforcing a code in which girls would not be treated differently than boys, students of color would not be stereotyped, and gay, lesbian, bisexual, and transgender students would not be harassed. And indeed, they seemed committed to prohibiting such behaviors. However, they did not often share my beliefs that oppression played out in other ways and that they therefore needed to do more to challenge oppression. On the contrary, they would quite passionately say that they should not do more to challenge oppression, lest they be seen as "too political" or as "imposing" on their students their own beliefs about social issues. The classroom should be a neutral place, neither oppressive nor anti-oppressive. In fact, although they seemed willing to include diverse experiences and perspectives in the curriculum, they suggested that such calls for political correctness were preventing them from teaching academic materials without bias.

In response, I started designing lessons to challenge the myth of "non"-oppressive teaching. Part II of this book will examine a number of ways that oppression is already playing out in various disciplines. But here I wish to emphasize that, regardless of the subject matter and even with the youngest of students, our teaching cannot help but be infused with oppressive elements. In what follows, I describe a lesson I once used to teach about the unintentional aspects of our teaching, especially the unintentional ways that our teaching reinforces different forms of oppression.

UNINTENTIONAL WAYS OF TEACHING

The lesson occurred toward the beginning of a semester-long course for student teachers. I began the lesson by dividing the chalkboard in half, and I asked the students to brainstorm: When does gender matter or come up as an issue in schools? In other words, when do we learn something about gender? Going around the room, I asked each student to share at least one instance, recording their responses in two lists (Table 1).

• celebrating Women's History Month	• lining up for separate restrooms
• lessons on women writers	• more resources for boys athletics
• lessons on gender discrimination	• only girls can wear skirts
• prohibiting sexist name-calling	• sitting boy-girl-boy-girl
• guest speaker on transgenderism	• boys play here, girls play there
• discussing one's same-gender partner	• separation during sex education
	• boys team versus girls team
	• calling on girls less
	• asking boys to move heavy items
	• saying good girls don't act "like that"
	• encouraging boys to take science
	• cross-dressing during Halloween
	• boy-girl couples at dances
	• boy-girl couples on prom courts
	• calling boys a "sissy girl"
	• more women teachers in elem school
	• more male figures in textbooks
	• more literature by male authors
	• saying "Mr." or "Ms."
	• forms for "mother or father"

I then asked, What are some differences between these two lists? Students observed many differences. The right-hand list is longer. Many of the right items take place all the time while the left items are very infrequent. The right items often go unobserved because they have become commonplace in schools, whereas the left items often stand out for the ways they challenge the norms of schools. The right items are often unintentional ways of teaching. And because they are so pervasive, everyday, and rarely challenged, the right items are more likely to shape what students come to believe is the way things are or are supposed to be. Thus, occasional lectures about the importance of treating girls in the same ways as boys will mean little if students observe that the teacher calls on boys to move tables and girls to sweep, that the text-book teaches about men in history more than about women, that dress codes require different clothing from boys than from girls, and that the hall monitor fails to challenge the sexist name-calling that happens constantly in the hallways. The intentional lessons on gender stand little chance in countering the unintentional ones.

Why is this a problem? Because the right items tend to be more negative, putting people into boxes or hierarchies, as when they reinforce the notions that there are exactly two genders, that males are quite different than females, and that males are more valued than females. In other words, the right items tend to reinforce the oppressive ideas of gender that many students have already learned in their everyday lives. These unintentional lessons make up the "hidden" curriculum of oppression that permeates our schools and that complicates any movement to reform curriculum and teach toward social justice. I am not suggesting that we forego the types of lessons on the left-hand column. However, challenging oppression cannot simply involve adding such lessons to our curriculum; it cannot simply involve changing what we intentionally teach. Challenging oppression must also involve addressing the many ways that we unintentionally teach; it requires illuminating and raising questions about the messages that are communicated by virtue of the very ways we operate schools. The process of teaching involves not only what we do but also what we do not do, what we say as well as what we do not say, what we include as well as what we do not include, how we interact as well as how we do not interact. We can never teach in ways that do not involve hidden lessons, especially hidden lessons that reflect the oppressive norms of society.

The hidden lessons are not always oppressive. Quite often, our unintentional lessons can be quite affirming or liberating. In fact, our unintentional lessons are quite often contradictory, communicating several messages at the same time. It is possible for the same teaching moment to communicate both oppressive and anti-oppressive messages. And this is what makes addressing the hidden curriculum so difficult: We can never know exactly what students are learning.

To practice recognizing the multiplicitous and contradictory nature of the hidden curriculum, I followed the brainstorming activity with two video clips of teachers teaching. Both clips showed teachers intentionally challenging oppression. I asked my students to suggest a range of possible hidden messages that students in the classrooms might be learning. One clip featured an elementary classroom during a "show and tell" activity. With many students waving electronic games in the air, the teacher teased that these games were dull, and looked for someone with something unusual to show. When the teacher turned to one boy to ask what he brought, the boy excitedly pulled from his bag two dolls that resembled Barbie and Ken. Classmates began to laugh, but the teacher quickly quieted them and said there was nothing wrong with liking the dolls. The teacher asked the boy if he wanted to be like the male doll, and joked that he would make a cute couple with a female classmate, who also brought the dolls. Classmates giggled, and the teacher proceeded to turn the class's attention to the toy brought by another student.

Some of my students suggested that, in this moment, it was possible for the students to learn that boys do not have to act in ways that we think boys are "supposed" to act, but can participate in activities usually associated with girls (playing with dolls). On the other hand, some of my students suggested that it was possible for the students to learn that boys do have to act in certain ways, in particular, by entering male-female romantic relationships. Some of my students suggested that, because the teacher wanted to see things other than the popular electronic games, it was possible for the students to learn that they do not have to follow the norm. On the other hand, some of my students suggested that, because the teacher assumed that boys would identify with the male doll, it was possible for students to learn that they do have to follow the norm. Some of my students suggested that it was possible for the boy who brought the dolls to learn that the teacher did not care about him since she did not let him explain why he liked the dolls, but that it was also possible for the boy to learn that the teacher did care about him since she diverted attention away from him in this uncomfortable situation.

The second video clip featured a high school English classroom during a short lesson on grammar. Students were to correctly identify the parts of speech in the sentence on the chalkboard, and the teacher threw candy to the students who answered correctly. Students were playful and rowdy, and when they came to identify the word "homeboy," they began pointing to themselves and to one another, teasing each other and strutting about proudly. A few minutes into the lesson, when students used vulgar language to complain about the lesson (including sexually demeaning language toward the teacher), the teacher responded with sarcastic humor and refocused their attention. The teacher then presented them with a poetry assignment, reasoning that, if they could read poetry, they could read anything. As an incentive, the teacher explained that, after they completed the assignment, she would take them on a trip to the amusement park, paid for by the school district. The students cheered, expressing some disbelief, and they began analyzing the poem.

Some of my students suggested that, because the teacher extolled the virtues of poetry, it was possible for the students to learn that learning is valuable in and of itself. On the other hand, it was also possible for the students to learn that learning is valuable when it comes with material rewards like candy or field trips. Some of my students suggested that, because the teacher did not reprimand them, it was possible for the students to learn that vulgar language was acceptable. However, because the teacher responded with humor and sarcasm and kept the lesson moving, it was also possible for the students to learn that vulgar language was not acceptable. Some of my students suggested that, because the sentence on the board had to do with "homeboys," and because the teacher participated in their play on words, it was possible for the students to learn that education can be connected to their own lives. However, because classic English poetry and expensive amusement parks were not things the students typically experienced, it was also possible for the students to learn that education can be about escaping their own lives.

Clearly, the students in the clips could have been learning things that exceeded what the teachers intended to teach, including things that directly contradicted the teachers' goals. But it is not possible to say exactly what the students were learning. And therein lies the uncertainty of teaching.

TEACHING WITH UNCERTAINTY

What students learn depends significantly on the unique lenses they use to make sense of their experiences. In other words, the ways that students have already learned to make sense of and feel about themselves and their world influences what and how they learn the things taught in school. In chapter 2, I suggested that these lenses can influence what students learn from our *intended* curriculum. For example, students might be more open to learning a theme in a novel because it reflected something they experienced earlier in life, or might be more open to learning about a certain property in earth science because they had already been wondering about such things. Or, students might be less open to learning about, say, religious differences because they feel that they already know the correct ways to think about spirituality, or they might be able to understand religious differences only in ways that adhere to what they already learned from their family.

Similarly, these lenses can influence what students learn from our *unintended* curriculum. For example, when a teacher calls on boys more than on girls, we can imagine a range of student responses. Some students might conclude—at either a conscious or subconscious level—that the teacher dislikes girls; other students might conclude that the teacher thinks those particular boys are the most learned; still others might conclude that the teacher is calling on those boys in an effort to focus their short attention span. Similarly, we can imagine different ways that students might understand a teacher's failing to discipline a student who tells a boy to stop walking "like a girl." Some might conclude that the teacher thinks there is nothing wrong with saying such things; others might conclude that the teacher is afraid to say anything because that teacher does not want to call attention to the teacher's own gender nonconformity; still others might conclude that the teacher wants to help but not in a way that draws more attention to the boy.

Several factors can influence what students learn in such situations, and these factors can operate simultaneously and subconsciously. Some students might view the teacher's action or inaction as part of a pattern. Perhaps the teacher had always called on boys more than girls, or had previously remained silent when students name-call, or had said things before that suggested that the teacher only calls on students who are smart, or who are playing around, or whom they like, or whom they wish to make an example of. Some students might view the teacher's action/inaction as responsive to the unique situation in which it was observed. Perhaps the teacher was aware of the presence of a homophobic administrator, or had just given a lesson on ways that students need to stick up for one another, or gave a certain glance that suggested that something would happen later.

And some students might simply view the teacher's action/inaction as reinforcing what they have learned about gender elsewhere. Perhaps the observing student already felt that boys are naturally smarter than girls and thus concluded that the teacher is rightfully calling on boys more. Perhaps the student had previous teachers who privileged boys and thus concluded that the teacher is yet another example of sexism in action. Perhaps the student already felt that boys are supposed to be "masculine" and thus concluded that there was no need for the teacher to respond to the sexist comment. Perhaps the student had previously been teased for not behaving in gender-appropriate ways and thus felt that the teacher was, as usual, failing to protect students. Students can see or conclude very different things, depending on their life experiences, values, and identities.

So what does this all mean for teaching? As my students and I concluded the discussion of the video clips, we debated the implications of these ideas. Some students felt that teaching is quite impossible. If we acknowledge that students will always learn different things from one another and even from what we intended to teach, what is the point of designing curriculum and of trying to tailor the curriculum to individual students? Other students felt that teaching simply needs to be done more conscientiously. If we acknowledge that our unintentional lessons often contradict our intentional lessons and, more importantly, that our unintentional lessons often reflect the status quo, shouldn't we simply teach more carefully in order to rid our classrooms of unintentional lessons?

My response was to encourage a radical rethinking of what it means to teach. Yes, teaching is impossible, but only if we believe that teaching is successful when students learn exactly what we said beforehand that they were supposed to learn. Were we to define teaching as a process that not only gives students the knowledge and skills that matter in society, but also asks students to examine the political implications of that knowledge and skills, then we should expect that there will always be more to our teaching than what we intended. We should expect that our teaching cannot help but to have hidden lessons (since "examining political implications" requires searching for the hidden messages that cannot help but exist in our classroom). This also means that, Yes, teaching requires being careful and conscientious, but the goal is not to rid our classroom of harmful hidden messages since such a goal is unattainable. Rather, the goal is to conscientiously make visible these hidden lessons and the various lenses students use to make sense of them. After all, our hidden lessons demonstrate how it is that oppression can play out in our lives unnoticed and unchallenged, and our lenses of analysis demonstrate why it is that we often desire making sense of the world in only certain, comforting ways. They are not barriers to anti-oppressive education; rather, they are what help to make anti-oppressive education possible. We need to be examining our lessons and lenses, their political implications, and possible alternatives. Ironically, we need to put front and center the very things we do not want in our teaching, the very things we do not even know are in our teaching.

The chapters in Part II of this book will illustrate some of the hidden lessons and other uncertainties involved in teaching various disciplines. The chapters will also suggest some of the ways that students might respond differently to these lessons, given their different lenses of analysis. But first I turn to chapter 4, which examines why teachers are not often learning about hidden curriculums or developing alternative lenses while in teacher education programs. I suggest that the movements that currently characterize teacher education make disturbingly little use of uncertainty.

QUESTIONS FOR REFLECTION AND DISCUSSION

1. (Comprehension) What are similarities and differences between the formal curriculum and the hidden curriculum, and what are aspects of schools that "teach" each curriculum?
2. (Comprehension) What are possible examples in schools of the formal curriculum and the hidden curriculum on race, and to what extent do these examples reflect your own schooling experiences?
3. (Concretization) If one goal of teaching is to raise awareness of and critique the hidden curriculum in whatever lesson is being taught, what might the content and structure of that lesson look like (for a given topic and grade level), and how might this be done in a way that addresses curriculum standards and high-stakes assessments?
4. (Critique) How should teachers address the hidden curriculum if they acknowledge that students come to school with multiple "lenses" that influence what and how they learn in unpredictable ways?

SAMPLING OF NEW RESOURCES

For analyses of curriculum development and curriculum theory:

- Marshall, J. D., Sears, J. T., Allen, L. A., Roberts, P. A., & Schubert, W. H. (2006). *Turning Points in Curriculum: A Contemporary American Memoir*, 2nd Edition. New York: Prentice Hall.
- Slattery, P. (2006). *Curriculum Development in the Postmodern Era*, 2nd Edition. New York: Routledge.

For analyses of hidden curriculum on cultural differences and ability differences:

- Gonzalez, N., Moll, L. C., & Amanti, C. (2005). *Funds of Knowledge: Theorizing Practices in Households, Communities, and Classrooms*. Mahwah, NJ: Lawrence Erlbaum Associates.
- Sapon-Shevin, M. (2007). *Widening the Circle: The Power of Inclusive Classrooms*. Boston: Beacon Press.

For analyses of teaching towards social justice while addressing curriculum standards:

- Sleeter, C. E. (2005). *Un-Standardizing Curriculum: Multicultural Teaching in the Standards-Based Classroom*. New York: Teachers College Press.

4

PREPARING TEACHERS FOR HEALING:
A CONVERSATION WITH BUDDHISM

ON AN EARLY SUNDAY MORNING in the middle of spring, a student at the college where I was teaching was stabbed to death on the outskirts of campus. The media framed the tragedy as a conflict between college and town, and the college seemed to mourn as much the loss of life as the loss of any sense of an idyllic existence. Come Monday morning, in the midst of much grief and unease, classes continued as usual. By Tuesday afternoon, when students came to my class, they had much to say about the responses of the faculty, who for the most part seemed to treat teaching and learning as processes that do not and perhaps should not address what happens in their daily lives. Not unlike the days following the tragic attacks on the United States on September 11th, 2001, professors adhered to their syllabi, and to learn, students needed to quickly put aside their emotions. Their courses had already been planned in the abstract, with topics and assignments that proceeded rationally from one to the next, forming a coherent set of lessons that would help students learn what the faculty already decided needed to be learned. Addressing the realities of the here and now was a departure from teaching that many faculty did not and/or could not take.

As I listened to my students, I found myself revisiting earlier conversations with colleagues about how to reform teacher education. Teacher education programs often require students to take courses that aim to provide students with a base or foundation of knowledge and skills that align with state and national standards of what future teachers need to know and be able to do. I remember expressing profound discomfort at the idea that there are "foundations" to teacher education and that through the required set of courses, all student teachers will learn these foundations. I noted that the necessary knowledge and skills of teacher education seem pre-defined, ordered, and fixed, as exemplified in our tendencies to use syllabi from year to year with little or no changes of the "classics." Teacher education, like the rest of the academy, does not seem to acknowledge the partial nature of what it requires students to learn, and in consequence, often remains disconnected from the everyday lived realities of students.

When my students asked about alternative ways to structure curriculum, I pointed to an example of an education course taught several years earlier by one of my mentors that was designed in response to racial tension on campus in the semester preceding. In that course, students were learning theories and practices of education within the context of a problem to solve, namely, racism on their campus. The course did not purport to teach foundations of education; rather, it made explicit that what was taught and learned was necessarily partial, was already framed by its sociohistorical context, and was useful for only certain political and pedagogical purposes. Although I could imagine critics saying that this course was too political and did not give students an objective study of education, I suggested to my students that courses are always partial and political, and that this course not only made that explicit, but also defined a partial, political problem on which all of its teachings and learnings were centered. I wondered aloud, What would teacher education look like if all its courses were structured in this way?

In my search for a theoretical framework that could help me imagine this restructured teacher education, I came across writings in Buddhism, especially an activist strand of Buddhism known as "socially engaged Buddhism." Practitioners of this strand of Buddhism apply their religion when addressing social, political, economic, and ecological problems, taking to heart the urgings of Vietnamese Buddhist monk Thich Nhat Hanh to engage in or practice Buddhist teachings in our daily lives. When turning to applications in the realm of education, I was particularly intrigued by Nhat Hanh's characterization of teachers as "healers." I was not interested in developing a form of education that teaches students to become Buddhist. Rather, I wanted to know, What might socially engaged Buddhism tell us about teaching and learning against oppression?

The Buddhist religion, with origins dating back twenty-five centuries to South Asia, is not unlike other religions in that it has many strands across the world, and throughout history has been used to both contribute to and challenge various forms of oppression. Buddhism provides neither one answer, nor *the* answer, to the question of how to restructure teacher education. It does, however, offer insights that educational research has yet to significantly engage. Common to different strands of Buddhism is the goal of understanding and reducing suffering in our lives, which is possible only when people relate to the world in very different ways. According to Buddhism, life in this world involves suffering. And people suffer because they attribute meaning and substance and value to knowledge, signs, and representations of reality rather than to reality itself.

Relating to the world through our knowledge can lead to suffering for two reasons. First, the knowledge of the world that we have produced is a knowledge centered on binaries, such as of self and other, inner and outer, us and them, means and ends, win or lose. Such binaries are problematic not only for reinforcing hierarchies of one party over another, but also for excluding third parties, as when binaries of, say, male and female make sense only because other, intersexed genders have been excluded. Since our languages and knowledge always and already operate within a binary logic, such hierarchies and exclusions are inescapable. Second, the knowledge of the world that we have produced often leads us to falsely believe that things in this world are permanent (unchanging) and independent (unconnected to other things). Such beliefs are problematic because they lead us to believe that we know the meaning of different things without acknowledging that things can mean different things in different situations, and that these meanings have everything to do with their relationships with one another. How we make sense of the world often "makes sense" only within a particular context and we should never feel comfortable that our knowledge will make sense in every context thereafter. The world will always exceed our knowledge of it.

Despite its problematic nature, we often cling to knowledge, perhaps because we have learned to find comfort in its everydayness or common sense, or perhaps because we see that the accumulation and reproduction of official knowledge matter in schools and society. Success in society, from job success to social prestige, often results from knowing or being able to do certain kinds of things. Success in schools in the form of grades and awards also results from knowing or being able to do certain kinds of things. We have learned that having certain kinds of knowledge matters in schools and society, and it is hard to let go.

For Nhat Hanh, learning is not about acquiring more knowledge. Learning is about releasing our dependence on knowledge that has, until now, framed the ways we live in this world. In other words, central to the processes of teaching and learning is addressing the limitations of how we teach and learn and what we know and are coming to know. Even the Buddhist teachings are limited and are merely tools that themselves eventually need to be abandoned and let go. This does not mean that the goal is to get rid of the wrong knowledge and find the right one since all knowledge is partial and limiting. Nor does this mean that the goal is a state of total ignorance, which is impossible since we already have knowledge and always produce and reproduce more. Rather, the goal is to treat knowledge paradoxically: use it in ways that help us improve our lives, but constantly interrupt the suffering that results from how we learn and what we think.

As teachers and students, the process of troubling the knowledge that we have produced and continue to produce can be very discomforting, not only because it departs from commonsensical notions of what it means to teach and learn, but also because it challenges each of us to complicate the ways we make sense of ourselves and the world in which we live. As teacher educators, the process of troubling the foundations of "becoming a teacher" can be similarly discomforting when we find ourselves departing from commonsensical discourses of what it means to prepare teachers to teach. Yet, this troubled, paradoxical relationship with knowledge and teaching and learning is perhaps exactly what can help us work toward anti-oppressive change.

The insights of Nhat Hanh invite me to imagine very different approaches to teacher education. I can imagine, for example, courses that center on addressing social problems in the here and now, rather than on abstracted orderings of what someone has already defined to be the things future teachers need to learn. I can imagine programs that strive to prepare teachers who relate to the world and to knowledge in very troubled, paradoxical ways, rather than in ways that value the accumulation of what someone has already defined to be valuable. I can imagine teacher educators who care about teachers and students working to reduce suffering, rather than conforming to commonsensical ideals of who they are supposed to be and become. And I imagine that such aspects of teacher education can help us address our students who are suffering from tragedies or from just living in this world.

QUESTIONS FOR REFLECTION AND DISCUSSION

1. (Comprehension) According to socially engaged Buddhism, how does knowledge connect with suffering, and what does it mean to "let go" of knowledge?
2. (Concretization) What would teaching and learning look like if they focused not on accumulating knowledge, or on dismissing knowledge, but on the process of "letting go" of knowledge?
3. (Critique) How might other philosophies, religions, and cultural traditions invite alternative ways of thinking about the relationship between knowledge, suffering, justice, and education?

SAMPLING OF NEW RESOURCES

For analyses of socially engaged Buddhism on suffering, knowledge, and justice:

- Nhat Hanh, T. (2007). *Buddha Mind, Buddha Body: Walking Toward Enlightenment.* Berkeley, CA: Parallax.
- Nhat Hanh, T. (2008). *The Art of Power.* New York: HarperOne.
- Nhat Hanh, T. (2009). *Thundering Silence: Sutra on Knowing the Better Way to Catch a Snake.* Berkeley, CA: Parallax.

5

PREPARING TEACHERS FOR ACTIVISM:
A REFLECTION ON THINGS QUEER

THE ACTIVISM THAT DRIVES "socially engaged Buddhism" raises the question, What could it mean to define the group "teachers," especially anti-oppressive teachers, as activists? There are many types of activists, some who work to reinforce the privilege of certain groups or perspectives in society, and others who work to challenge it. Of the many forms of activism that challenge oppression, there is not one best form. However, given my earlier critique of common sense, I do find myself particularly drawn to forms of activism that seek to change what has become normalized in society. That is, I find myself drawn to the forms of activism that address how certain things become defined as normal and all other things as not normal or "queer." How might theories and examples of "queer" activism inform our movement toward anti-oppressive change?

We often think of the word "queer" as a very hurtful, negative word. Indeed, "queer" was and still often is a word used to draw attention to the ways people are not "normal," especially in terms of sexual orientation (as with people who are gay, lesbian, bisexual), gender identity (people who are transgender, intersexual), or even gender expression (boys who act "like girls," girls who look "like boys," those we simply "can't tell"). We say, "They're so queer" as an insult, "I'm not queer" as a defense, "That's so queer" as a joke, or simply "Queer!" to accompany an act of physical violence. We learn not to like people or things that are queer. We learn not to want to be queer.

51

Some people who identify themselves as gay, lesbian, bisexual, transgender, and intersexed seem to agree that being queer is bad and respond by showing that they are as normal as everyone else. But other people respond by explaining that, Yes, they are not what society defines as normal, and more importantly, that they do not want to be normal because being normal is a pretty oppressive way to be. Being normal is not unlike doing what is common sense. Both require conforming to what some in society have said are the ways that we are supposed to be. Being normal requires thinking in only certain ways, feeling only certain things, and doing only certain things. And it punishes those who do not conform, such as those who do not look normal, or love the right kind of person, or value the important things. Society's definition of normalcy, as with society's understanding of common sense, teaches us not only to conform to an oppressive status quo, but also to actually want to conform. Activists who reject this imperative to conform often celebrate the ways that they are queer. They tell us that being queer is not a bad thing at all. They tell us that they are changing the word queer to mean something empowering and disruptive. They tell us, in other words, that being "queer" is perhaps exactly what can help society move toward social justice.

Certainly, the word "queer" continues to be a very troubling word, even among those committed to social justice, and especially in an educational context. Perhaps one reason that addressing queer issues is a difficult process is because we often search for comfortable ways to do this work. This leads me to wonder, What would happen if we explored approaches to social justice that were premised on being uncomfortable? The field of education has not often concerned itself with insights from queer activism in exploring what it means to challenge oppression. Some educators might assume that drawing on queer activism means teaching students to identify with queer sexualities and genders. This is not how I am suggesting that we use queer activism to rethink education. Just as my discussion of Buddhism did not say that we should be teaching students to be Buddhist, so too does my discussion of queer activism not say that we should be teaching students to be sexually queer. Rather, I am interested in seeing what we can learn when we examine some of the ways that queer activism conceptualizes oppression and social justice. There are many forms and aspects of queer activism, each with different strengths and weaknesses, which means that queer activism is not *the* answer to our problems. However, I do believe that it can suggest ways of thinking that go beyond common sense.

Queer activists often work to expose problems in the status quo and help us imagine and create more socially just alternatives. They work to change laws and policies by lobbying legislators or staging protests, they teach others to break through glass ceilings or challenge discriminatory employment or housing or healthcare practices, and they organize community or school groups for political action. And as they teach us to become dissatisfied and uncomfortable with the norms of society, they ask us to examine why we have already become uncomfortable with the "queers" of society. They ask us to confront the discomfort we feel when seeing outrageous performers in pride parades, or when learning about homophobia in certain courses, or when talking about "out" friends and family members. By insisting that queer things be visible in parades or courses or everyday conversations, queer activists seem to be insisting that we ask ourselves such questions as, Why are we comfortable with closeted queers but not with visibly queer queers? Why are we comfortable with lessons on homophobia in some contexts but not in others? Why are we comfortable with queer acquaintances but not queer loved ones? Queer activists seem to suggest that changing how we think about and treat queers involves addressing what we already know about queers and why we feel comfortable relearning only certain things.

Like queer activism, teacher education needs to involve challenging both the institutional practices that perpetuate an oppressive norm and our emotional responses to and discomfort with things that are queer. As I suggested in the previous chapters, certain practices in teacher education are often considered to be quite queer, especially those that do not reflect what we believe we are supposed to be doing. As we learn very different ways of teaching and learning, we might ask: What would teacher education look like if we placed a priority on examining why we feel comfortable with only certain kinds of teaching? Why do certain teaching practices feel like they are not "real" teaching? Why do certain teaching practices result in students' learning things that they feel are not what they are supposed to be learning? How might the queer ways of teaching and the queer things we are learning suggest very different ways of making sense of ourselves and our world? How does calling these teachings and learnings "queer" help and hinder our efforts to work toward social justice?

One reason I like the term *queer* is that it reminds me never to stop asking, What is problematic with the norm? People working toward social justice often reach a point when they think they have arrived at the best approaches to achieve their goals. What was once the alternative suddenly becomes the norm, and what was once queer suddenly becomes quite comforting. However, no approach is unproblematic, which means that no approach can ever be *the* way to solve our problems. Queer activists remind me that we must continue to ask how our practices contribute to oppression. We must be open to confronting the uncomfortable realization that our anti-oppressive approaches, like all approaches, define other approaches as queer. When we challenge racism, what approaches to challenging sexism (including sexism among people of color) get silenced? When we challenge sexism, what approaches to challenging classism get excluded? When we challenge classism, what approaches to challenging racism get subsumed? We should not be comfortable repeating what, at one point, we considered to be queer. Rather, we must always look to what we are indirectly defining as the new queer things in our teaching. Learning to teach toward social justice involves constantly engaging with the things that make whatever we are doing uncomfortable and queer.

What is significant here is queer theory's focus on the *production* of queerness. Some things could not be normal (like opposite-sex attraction) if other things were not already abnormal (like same-sex attraction). Queerness is not a natural state of being. Rather, queerness is produced as a contrast, as that against which normalcy is established. Within teacher education, the norms include both the commonsensical practices and the reformed practices that have now become commonly accepted in teacher education programs. Queer theory tells us that these norms actually *produce* queerness. By saying that *this* is what is means to be a teacher/learner, the field of teacher education is simultaneously saying that other images of teacher/learner are pretty queer. By saying that teaching/learning is supposed to look *like this* (i.e., neutral, objective, bias-free), the field of teacher education simultaneously is saying that all other ways of teaching/learning (including nonneutral, anti-oppressive ways) are pretty queer.

Not surprisingly, oppression (in both schools and society) is difficult to change. Challenging oppression requires more than simply becoming aware of oppression, and this is because people are often *invested* in the status quo, as when people desire repeating what has become normalized in our lives. Change requires a willingness to step outside of this comfort zone. And for those who are favored by or benefit from the status quo, change may be even more difficult since it requires interrupting one's own privilege. There is a range of reasons—political, psychosocial—explaining why people might resist change. Thus, within schools, students often resist acknowledging the oppressiveness of their everyday identities and practices, teachers often resist acknowledging the oppressiveness of common teaching practices, and teacher educators often resist acknowledging the oppressiveness of even reformed teacher education curriculum. Disrupting the normalcy of certain ways of teaching (and the queerness of other ways) requires addressing these resistances and the discomfort that results.

Indeed, perhaps the most significant way that anti-oppressive teaching is queer is its use of discomfort or crisis. Common definitions of "good" teaching often leave little, if any, room for the moments in education when confronting one's own resistances to disruptive knowledge can be traumatic. In fact, "good" teaching often means that crisis is averted, that lessons are doable and comfortable, that problems are solved, that learning results in feeling better, that knowledge is a good thing. This is the case even within some approaches to teaching that aim to raise awareness of oppression through rational discussion and analysis. Yet, if anti-oppressive teaching requires disrupting the repetition of comforting knowledges, then students will always need to confront what they desire not to confront. And since learning what we desire not to learn (as when learning that the very ways in which we think, identify, and act are not only partial but also problematic) can be an upsetting process, crisis should be expected in the process of learning, by both the student and the teacher. Like queer activism, queer teaching always *works through* crisis. And like queer activism, the goal is not to be able to teach without crisis. The absence of crisis signals that queerness has become normalized, that the experience of queerness is no longer so different, and therefore, that queerness itself (at least, what was previously considered queer) has become normative. Rather, the goal is to continue teaching and learning through crisis—to continue experiencing the queer.

QUESTIONS FOR REFLECTION AND DISCUSSION

1. (Comprehension) When does activism become "queer" activism, and what would make education a form of queer activism?
2. (Concretization) What aspects of education have become normalized, what aspects are today considered quite "queer," and what does it mean to teach in way that is designed to "continue experiencing the queer"?
3. (Critique) What are other forms of activism besides queer activism, and what are strengths and weaknesses of each form in advancing social justice when compared with queer activism?

SAMPLING OF NEW RESOURCES

For analyses of queer theory in education:

- Meyer, E. J. (2009). *Gender, Bullying, and Harassment: Strategies to End Sexism and Gender, Bullying, and Harassment.* New York: Teachers College Press.
- Rasmussen, M. L., Rofes, E., & Talburt, S. (2004). *Youth and Sexualities: Pleasure, Subversion, and Insubordination In and Out of Schools.* New York: Palgrave Macmillan.
- Rofes, E. (2005). *A Radical Rethinking of Sexuality and School: Status Quo or Status Queer?* Boulder, CO: Rowman & Littlefield.

For analyses of activism and education:

- Ellsworth, E. (2004). *Places of Learning: Media, Architecture, Pedagogy.* New York: Routledge.
- Pinar, W. F. (2009). *The Worldliness of a Cosmopolitan Education: Passionate Lives in Public Service.* New York: Routledge.

II

PREPARING ANTI-OPPRESSIVE TEACHERS
IN SIX DISCIPLINES

IN THE CHAPTERS THAT FOLLOW, I explore implications of the concepts discussed in Part I for six disciplines: social studies, English literature,
music, "foreign" languages, the natural sciences, and mathematics. I do
not purport to present *the* anti-oppressive way to think about and
teach these disciplines. I do not attempt to suggest how to revise the
entire curriculum within a discipline. Rather, I focus on one topic
within the discipline, and I examine how the theories in Part I suggest
different ways of teaching that topic. I draw on lessons that I have
taught for elementary, middle, and secondary school students, I imagine alternative ways that I could have taught them, and then I reflect on
the different political implications of each approach. As I do so, I
examine what it might mean to prepare teachers to teach such lessons,
and I discuss possible reasons why such preparation can be difficult.

These chapters are not blueprints for best practices; they are not
meant to be duplicated in other programs and classrooms. Admittedly,
they present somewhat simplified examples to make each discipline
accessible to a very broad readership. And, as suggested at the end of
each chapter, all the examples presented have strengths and weaknesses. They do, however, model the kind of design and analysis that I
believe is suggested by theories of anti-oppressive education. Readers
are encouraged to think of these chapters as case studies in anti-
oppressive teacher education and to imagine what additional examples

might look like in their own classroom. These chapters present examples of the kinds of perspectives and practices made possible when we apply theories from Part I to particular, unique, context-bound moments in our teaching. What we can learn from these chapters is how to take a lesson from our curriculum and rethink its oppressive tendencies and anti-oppressive possibilities. Our goal is not to completely revise our curriculum so that it is fully anti-oppressive. Rather, our goal is to take one lesson or topic or moment at a time, apply some theories of anti-oppressive education, and then see what teaching, learning, and changes are made possible.

6

EXAMPLES FROM SOCIAL STUDIES

My EXPERIENCES suggest that it is often easier to imagine anti-oppressive changes in social studies curriculums than in the curriculums of other disciplines. Many of the discussions I have heard about trying to make curriculum more inclusive or multicultural (or about resisting a move toward "political correctness") often revolve around social studies, especially the study of U.S. history. Perhaps this is because, more than other disciplines, social studies focuses on teaching and learning about the aspects of our lives that we associate primarily with issues of oppression, namely, the social aspects of our lives, including how we identify, how we interact with one another, and how we experience the world around us, both historically and today. Although the later chapters in this book will suggest that other disciplines can each make unique and significant movements toward social justice, it is certainly the case that social studies is well suited to teach about the oppressive tendencies and anti-oppressive possibilities of different ways of making sense of our identities, cultures, institutions, and histories.

Already, many educators are changing the nature of social studies by moving away from curriculums that merely repeat the stories we have traditionally told about, say, U.S. history. They tell us, rightfully so, that including the experiences and perspectives of only certain people in the United States teaches that only certain people matter in society, historically and today. In an attempt to tell a story that reflects more of the diversity of U.S. society, they have added materials and raised questions that point to the experiences and perspectives and contributions of people who have traditionally been marginalized in society. These people include women, people of color, the working classes, people from different religious backgrounds, and people with different sexual orientations.

In an effort to build on this movement, I suggest that educators can do even more to change the nature of social studies and teach toward social justice. Diversifying the curriculum is important, but as some educators have argued, teachers and students need to engage in a type of analysis that raises questions about whatever is included, even the new materials being added. To illustrate this point, I turn to what is often called the Second World War.

"SECOND WORLD WAR" AND SILENCES IN THE CURRICULUM

Lessons on World War II in U.S. history classes often focus on the oppressiveness of the regimes gaining control across Europe and Asia, their inhumane treatment of certain religious, ethnic, and other groups, and the work and eventual triumphs of U.S. and allied political leaders and military forces in toppling them. In response to what some have called the "greatest evil" of the twentieth century, the United States put forth what some have called its "greatest generation" to protect freedom and democracy around the world. Such a story helps us appreciate and admire the sacrifices of our older generations when helping to end the ways certain regimes were torturing and killing millions of people simply because they were different. Schools need to continue to teach such a story.

But there is much more that schools need to teach about the behavior of the United States during the war. Often silenced in or excluded from lessons on the war are the roles women played in transforming the workforce in the United States. With so many young men employed by the military, women were needed to fill roles in occupations traditionally reserved for men. Often silenced in lessons on the war are the forced relocation and internment of 120,000 Japanese Americans in the United States, many of whom were U.S. citizens. Unable to distinguish the "enemies" in Japan from the people who looked like the enemies in the United States, and unwilling to heed reports that claimed otherwise, the federal government concluded that Japanese Americans were a potential threat during the war and needed to be locked away in camps. Often silenced in lessons on the war is the persecution by Nazis of people who were gay, lesbian, or bisexual, as well as people simply accused of being so. Along with millions of Jews and other targeted groups, people who were identified as gay, lesbian, or bisexual were forced into concentration camps, but unlike other groups, they were often put back into prisons by U.S. troops who liberated the camps. Without including such information, lessons on the war simply retell the familiar narrative: The Nazis were evil for persecuting the innocent Jews, the United States was the force of good in the face of this evil, the men of the United States helped save the world, and women, gay/lesbian/bisexual people, and Japanese Americans were not heroes, victims, or otherwise.

It is certainly possible to include lessons on women, gay/lesbian/bisexual people, and Japanese Americans in ways that suggest that, Oh yes, they were also there. It should be noted, however, that including more experiences and perspectives may increase what we know about different groups in society but may not necessarily change the underlying story we tell about the United States. In contrast, it is also possible to include lessons on these groups in ways that draw attention to and raise questions about the underlying story. Questions we might ask include: Does the textbook implicitly teach us that the United States was the force of good and that we should celebrate the United States as the big brother to the world, the symbol of freedom and democracy? Does such a story allow us to forget the Japanese American internment camps and the ways that the United States perpetuated racism against its own citizens? Does such a story allow us to ignore the persecution of people with different sexual orientations and the ways that the United States reinforced homophobia at home (within the military) and abroad (by the military)? Does such a story teach us that "understanding history" involves understanding only those realms dominated by men? And does the inclusion of different experiences help us to critique such stories? Furthermore, does the inclusion of different experiences encourage us to pity a group? Or view a group as monolithic, or evil, or heroic, or in other ways one-dimensional and stereotypical?

Lessons that raise questions about the familiar stories we tell of the United States and its peoples can enable us to construct alternative stories that illuminate and disrupt the simplicity and oppression circulating in our nation's histories and identities. For example, we might conclude that, during the war, the United States acted in contradictory ways, challenging oppression on the basis of religion but contributing to oppression on the basis of race or sexual orientation. We might also conclude that the war prompted paradoxical changes in the United

States, disrupting the patriarchal division of labor while still centering the nation's identity and pride on the work of men. Why are such alternative stories important? Because different stories have different political implications: Some stories keep us blinded to or complicit with oppression, other stories urge us to challenge oppression, and still other stories affect us in other ways.

So, the task for teachers is not merely to add to the curriculum more information about different groups in society. The task is to ask questions about the political implications of the underlying story being told by whatever is included. What story about the United States (or whatever we are learning about) is suggested when these perspectives or experiences are included and when others are excluded? How does that story justify and/or challenge an oppressive status quo? When we add different perspectives, how does the story change or remain insidiously the same? How do different combinations of perspectives suggest different insights or identities or implications for social interaction? We need to examine how including and excluding different things tell different kinds of stories, and how the questions we ask or do not ask about those stories can make possible very different ways of making sense of our world, of ourselves, and of our obligations toward others.

These questions that help us to "look beyond" whatever it is that we are teaching and learning do not belong only in history classrooms. They also belong in the study of current events, and can help us to understand and challenge the contradictory and oppressive roles that the U.S. government currently plays around the world, including in another of its wars, the "war on terrorism."

"WAR ON TERRORISM" AND SILENCES IN THE MEDIA

I was sitting in my office on the morning of September 11, 2001, when a colleague rushed to my door to tell me that she had just heard that an airplane had crashed into one of the World Trade Center towers in New York City. As the hours passed, more airplanes crashed, both of the towers collapsed, a part of the Pentagon in Washington, D.C., was destroyed, and all attention seemed to turn to the terror that had hit U.S. soil. Thousands were presumed to have died, forthcoming tragedies were not ruled out, and the nation seemed paralyzed with grief, fear, and uncertainty. Classes were canceled at the college where I was teaching, so I headed home, glued to the radio and then the television. I, too, was overcome with sadness. I wept as I saw many die and heard many witnesses tell their stories of panic and loss. I, too, was overcome with fear. Some of the attackers passed through the airport not far from where I was then living, in Maine. I had friends and relatives living in New York City and Washington, D.C. I hoped that they were safe. And I hoped that I was safe.

Many people wanted answers. These were not tragic coincidences. These were planned attacks. Why would people want to attack "us"? How could people be so "evil"? Who is responsible? How will we punish "them"? Mixed in with grief, fear, and uncertainty was a profound sense of anger. I remember not being able to eat very much that day. My nausea was but one of the indications that I was, indeed, overcome with sadness and fear. But unlike many others, my feelings of sadness and fear resulted not only from acknowledging the attacks on U.S. soil and the deaths left in their wake. My feelings derived increasingly from how I suspected many in the United States would respond. News commentators were speculating that this was an act of terrorism by Muslim extremists, and political leaders were promising to use all at our disposal to punish those responsible for this "worst act of terrorism on U.S. soil." People wanted revenge. And I feared that in the name of revenge, many would be unwilling or even unable to recognize the oppressiveness of their responses. I feared that many would respond in terribly oppressive ways. Indeed, my fears were justified.

As U.S. intelligence agencies gathered evidence that "Muslim extremists" were responsible for these attacks, the responses were swift. Abroad, the United States sent more and more military forces to find and punish those responsible. Political leaders called for a war on terrorism that would span not only the Middle East but also the entire globe in an effort to eliminate those who sought to attack freedom and democracy. Within the United States, more and more individuals seemed to think this war was against anyone who "looked Muslim" or "looked Arab," including those who wore a turban or headwrap or simply had darker skin. Such Muslim-looking people were treated as potential criminals. They were carefully, even aggressively, scrutinized when trying to board airplanes and were subject to harassment and abuse. In the months that followed September 11th, the number of reports of hate incidences and hate crimes against individuals who looked Muslim increased dramatically in the United States. Although political leaders were quick to denounce such racial and religious scapegoating, they themselves were guilty of similar acts of harassment. As agencies responsible for fighting terrorism began arresting or harassing many they suspected of being connected to the attacks or to future attacks and were denying many of them of their constitutional rights, political leaders were granting more and more powers of surveillance to these agencies to fight terrorism. In fact, in an eerie parallel to the Japanese American internment during World War II, hundreds upon hundreds of people, including Muslim Americans and Americans of Middle Eastern descent, were rounded up and interned. These increased powers may have conflicted with our constitutional and civil rights, but polls indicated that the majority in the United States supported such a compromise.

This was, after all, a time for the nation to come together. We should stand behind our political leaders and present ourselves as a strong, united nation. We should be proud to be part of the United States and display this pride with flags on our shirts and our cars and our desks and our lawns. After all, the United States was said to symbolize freedom and democracy, and to attack the United States was to attack these institutions as well. The pressure to conform to these convictions was significant, as was the penalty for failing to do so. A politician who voiced dissent for the president's war policies received death threats. A teacher who challenged stereotypes of Muslims as crazed terrorists got accused of trying to convert students to Islam and was promptly fired. News that businesses were being attacked prompted at least one person of color who owned a business to demonstrate patriotism by hanging an extra large U.S. flag. News that individuals were being attacked verbally and physically for being "anti-American" prompted a woman and her partner to take down a sign from their apartment window that read "Give peace a chance." Being "American" required acting in only certain ways and wanting only certain things.

Schools often helped to reinforce such messages. More schools began saying the pledge of allegiance. Some political leaders called on students to sacrifice their own pocket change to donate to a fund to help the victims of the September 11th attacks, which teachers helped to collect. Some teachers asked students to work on projects that thanked or honored the relief workers at the sites of attack. Some classroom walls got covered in patriotic posters, and more classroom lessons included discussion of what it means to be a good citizen. Some teachers thanked President Bush, and God, for giving us the fortune of life in America. For some teachers, teaching toward social justice meant teaching students to honor what "America" stands for and to stand behind its war on terrorism.

Fortunately, many teachers were keenly aware that, in this time of heightened emotions, they needed to respond not by teaching simplistic and racist views of the attackers but by working explicitly to disrupt the racial and religious scapegoating that followed September 11th. For such teachers, teaching toward social justice meant teaching students about racial and religious differences and challenging stereotypes, particularly with regard to Islam. More and more social studies classrooms began incorporating such lessons, and some teachers changed their curriculums entirely in order to focus student learning on current events. I heard teachers say that they wanted students to learn that people who "look Muslim" come from many different backgrounds and ethnicities and hold a variety of different perspectives. They wanted students to understand that Islam is a peaceful religion and that the attackers were not "really" Muslim since they took Islamic ideas to the extreme. They wanted students to see that most of the people who "look Muslim" in the United States have nothing to do with the September 11th attackers. Such teachers understood that learning about racial and religious differences was important because students needed to see how the people being stereotyped and scapegoated were not like the people who attacked us. We do not say that all Christians bomb abortion clinics just because some do, so we should not say that all "Muslim-looking" people are terrorists just because some are.

Such lessons are important for the ways that they can help to create a less discriminatory society by helping students to understand differences and refrain from stereotyping. Such lessons can also strengthen a sense of togetherness by helping students to value our community and take pride in the ways we help one another in times of need. Schools need to continue to teach such things. However, there is much more that schools need to teach when working toward social justice in the face of "terrorism." There is much more that schools need to teach about the very ways we think about "terrorism." As with lessons on World War II, lessons on September 11th need to teach about the contradictory roles being played by the United States.

For example, lessons could critically analyze what the mainstream U.S. news media say and do not say, and the political implications of such messages. The media often say that by attacking the United States the "terrorists" were attacking freedom and democracy, and that they were extremists, unusual in their irrationality and inhumanity. What is not often said is many people around the world view the United States as a threat and even hindrance to their freedom, autonomy, and livelihood. They have seen the United States act through military campaigns, embargoes, financial endeavors, and political pressure, protecting its own financial self-interest in the name of protecting democracy. The result has been untold suffering as their countries or populations endured and continue to endure war, prolonged famine, brutal regimes, and loss of life throughout the world. Feeling exploited by Western capitalism, people around the world have staged protests against the United States, from Southeast Asia and the Pacific Islands to the southern tip of South America, from east African countries to Eastern European countries, and of course, even in the Middle East. It is not impossible to imagine that people can sometimes reach such a state of despair that they take their own lives and the lives of others to get the world to notice and make some changes. Although it is certainly possible that the attacks were attacks on freedom, it is also possible that the attacks were a desperate call for change in order to protect freedom. The blanket condemnation of the "terrorists" makes it easy to dehumanize the attackers and to call for punishments and retaliation, thus deflecting attention from our shared responsibility to make changes.

Of course, no one deserves to be killed or attacked in such a tragic way. The loss of life should not be excused or dismissed. But the attack was much more complicated than the story we often hear in the media and in schools. There is much about the United States that gets masked when we say that the "terrorists" were evil and deserve to be punished for attacking the United States. This is a partial story that allows us to continue ignoring ways that the United States contributes to the oppression of many others around the world.

Ironically, this partial story of "terrorists" gets told not only in lessons of teachers trying to create good citizens, but also in lessons of teachers trying to promote an appreciation for diversity. Teaching that many people who "look Muslim" are not like the "extremists" and therefore should not be scapegoated does not change the underlying assumptions that the "extremists" were evil and that the United States is the victim. As when teaching about World War II, teaching about September 11th cannot involve merely adding lessons about different groups of people. We need to be teaching students to ask questions about how the United States has acted and continues to act in contradictory ways. We need to be teaching about how politicians and the media often tell partial stories that allow us to continue understanding national and international events in only certain ways, especially in ways that reinforce common sense and the status quo. In other words, we need to expose and complicate even those stories our own curriculum unintentionally tells about Muslims, the United States, and oppression. And we need to raise questions about how those stories could change if we taught and learned different things about September 11th.

An anti-oppressive social studies curriculum is not purporting to tell *the* anti-oppressive story about September 11th, World War II, or whatever it is we are studying. Rather, it presents students with a range of materials and perspectives, including those perspectives that often matter in society, and then asks, What stories do these materials and perspectives seem to tell us, and what implications do these stories have for reinforcing as well as challenging the oppressive status quo?

LOOKING BEYOND: "WHY DID WE DO THIS?"

As often as I can, I try to acknowledge to my students the partial nature of what and how I am teaching. In my seminar for student teachers, one way I do this is by ending class sessions with several questions: Why did we do this? What could this teach? And what concerns might you have about this lesson? How might this lesson hinder our movement toward social justice? As I make explicit the ways in which I am trying to model different methods of teaching in each of our class sessions, I also try to make explicit that each method has strengths and weaknesses, including strengths and weaknesses of which not even I may be aware. As we reflect on these questions, my students often offer me new insights on my teaching, including insights on the multiple and contradictory hidden lessons that their varying lenses allow them to see.

Rarely have these reflections on my lessons left me content with my teaching. They may leave me feeling as though my students have gotten quite skillful at finding possible hidden messages and at recognizing the ways that my lessons involved choices and assumptions and underlying stories that both challenged and contributed to oppression. But they often leave me feeling as though I still have much to learn, even about things in which I claim to have expertise. For example, in my seminar with student teachers soon after September 11th, I taught a lesson about the hidden curriculum, and I asked them to use our seminar as the context in which to search for possible hidden lessons. A few days earlier, our class session had focused on ways that they as teachers might address tragedies such as September 11th in their own classrooms. As I pushed my students to suggest possible contradictory messages from that teaching moment, one student suggested that, on the surface, the lesson from a few days ago emphasized the importance of addressing tragedies in the lives of students and their emotional responses. However, beyond the surface, my lesson remained very theoretical and hypothetical. It did not address their own emotional responses and focused instead on how they as future teachers might respond to future tragedies with their students. Coming from a student teacher who did not say much in class that day, the comment left me concerned that I was not practicing what I was preaching.

I concluded class by explaining that their reflections suggested to me the importance of teaching with several questions always at the back of our minds: How might we plan lessons if we acknowledge that we can never accomplish everything we want to accomplish (because of limited time, because of unintentional hidden messages, because of the unpredictable lenses that students use)? How might a class discussion on these limitations invite students to look beyond these limitations (and how does a failure to discuss these limitations make it easier for students to feel that, once they learn the materials, their work is done)? I suggested that sometimes getting students to raise questions about what and how they are learning (as my students were doing with my lessons on September 11th and the hidden curriculum) can make possible a form of anti-oppressive education that always exceeds the intentions of the teacher … and that this can be a very liberating thing.

QUESTIONS FOR REFLECTION AND DISCUSSION

1. (Comprehension) How can a curriculum that is inclusive of diversity be problematic, that is, what might be the "hidden curriculum" of even inclusive curriculums?
2. (Comprehension) What are some examples of stories or perspectives that are often excluded from textbooks or from the media, why might this be so, and what are possible "hidden curriculums" that result from such exclusion?
3. (Concretization) What are various ways that you could organize, say, a U.S. history curriculum that would seek not only to be inclusive but also to address the partiality and contradictions of whatever is included?
4. (Critique) What skills or knowledge do students need in order to think critically about the hidden curriculum?

SAMPLING OF NEW RESOURCES

For analyses of social studies education:

- Ross, E. W. (Ed.). (2006). *The Social Studies Curriculum: Purposes, Problems, and Possibilities.* Albany, NY: SUNY Press.
- Wade, R. C. (2007). *Social Studies for Social Justice: Teaching Strategies for the Elementary Classroom.* New York: Teachers College Press.

For analyses of media education and popular education:

- Madedo, D., & Steinberg, S. R. (Eds.). (2007). *Media Literacy: A Reader.* New York: Peter Lang.
- McLaren, P., & Jaramilo, N. (2009). *Pedagogy and Praxis in the Age of Empire: Towards a New Humanism.* Rotterdam, The Netherlands: Sense Publishers.

7

EXAMPLES FROM ENGLISH LITERATURE

MORE AND MORE EDUCATORS are recognizing that teaching and learning English literature in ways that challenge oppression requires changing what we read. They tell us that students cannot only read the classics that have traditionally defined the best of British and U.S. literature. When students read literature by only certain groups of people, they learn about only certain experiences and perspectives, especially those of groups that have traditionally been privileged in society (such as White, middle-class men). The writings of different groups of people in this world can expose students to experiences and ideas different from their own. Such exposure is especially important when we ask students to find connections between the text and their own life experiences. A wider range of experiences and perspectives in the text might be able to engage students who do not normally see themselves in what they are reading. A wider range of texts might also present students with alternatives to the predominant or commonsensical ways of thinking that have traditionally framed or hindered the ways they make sense of their own lives.

Of course, writings from different groups of people can be problematic. Some writings can merely repeat stereotypes or create new ones by glossing over complexities, contradictions, and diversity, thereby suggesting that an entire culture or a group is *like this*. Other writings can include many complexities but still be read in simplified ways, such as when the reader pays attention to only certain stories being told. And in fact, as I suggested in Part I, readers often want to read only certain kinds of stories, perhaps because certain stories reinforce the ways that they have already learned to make sense of the world, or perhaps because certain stories present new information in a way that is grasp-able and accessible (instead of in ways that are complex, messy, and uncertain). Readers often subconsciously desire reading texts in com-forting ways, which is a problem since, as I will suggest in a moment, such comforting, simplified readings often carry oppressive political implications.

Therefore, in addition to changing what students read, educators are also changing *how* students read. It is not enough to expose students to a wider variety of literature if students continue to interpret or analyze the literature as has traditionally been done. Students need to be asking very different kinds of questions about whatever it is that they are read-ing. My own experiences are illustrative.

READING ABOUT RACISM

I once taught an English class in summer school for sixth graders. One of the books in the curriculum was Laurence Yep's *The Star Fisher,* a short novel about a Chinese American family moving from Ohio to West Virginia in the early 1900s. The novel details both the racism that the family encounters and the processes through which family mem-bers go as they form friendships with community members. Joan, the central character and the oldest daughter of the family, has an espe-cially difficult time balancing the more "traditional Chinese" perspec-tives of her parents with the more "American" perspectives of her peers. In this way, she is not unlike the central character of a Chinese folktale (after which the book is titled) who lives in two different worlds.

As we read this book, I remember asking different kinds of questions as I worked toward different goals. Some of my questions addressed factual issues and comprehension: Who was talking to whom, what event happened where and when, what does this word or phrase mean? The students in my class were just entering middle school, and my supervisor reminded me that one of the main goals of my course was to ensure that the students had the academic skills needed to succeed in high school. They needed to be able to understand what was going on in what they read.

Some of my questions focused on traditional topics of literary analy-sis, such as character development, plot, themes, and author's intent: Why did the parents feel a certain way about their neighbors? What event signaled a change in the way many community members received the family, and why might this have happened? How was the main character similar to the other "outcast" whom she befriended? What does this novel tell us about racism? What is the significance of the title, and what does it tell us about the main character? I wanted my students to learn to "see" the types of things that schools value when teaching and learning a novel, namely, the things that we deduce or induce when reading. And I wanted my students to see that some interpretations are often considered to be more correct. Occasionally, a student would offer an interpretation supported by details from the novel that differed from my own interpretation, and I would encourage such initiative and originality. However, I also felt that certain interpretations were more credible than others, and when in doubt, I sought consensus from my fellow teachers.

Some of my questions focused on the relevance of the novel to their own lives: Could they relate to the central character, to being an outcast, or to having conflicts with their parents? Have they ever treated a classmate as did the classmates of the central character? Have they befriended someone different from themselves? What experiences or observations of racism can they remember from their own lives? How would they have acted differently in the situation at the turning point of the novel? Would they have wanted to see a different ending? My goal, with such questions, was to help the students not only see connections between the novel and their own lives, but also internalize and grapple with some of the social issues with which the characters in the novel were grappling. My goal, in other words, was to make their experience reading the novel a personally meaningful one.

Such questions are certainly important to ask when teaching and learning literature. However, additional questions need to be asked. As I reflect on my lesson, I suspect that I likely taught hidden messages that reinforced the notion that only certain interpretations matter in schools and society. After all, I did not teach that we can find meanings in texts other than what we call the themes or character development. I did not teach that any interpretation uses particular lenses of analysis, including the interpretations that have come to be defined as neutral and objective. I did not teach that different lenses or interpretations can have different political implications. And I did not teach that, when we label certain lenses (including feminist lenses and anti-racist lenses) as too political, we are allowing other perspectives to remain invisible and, therefore, the norm (including perspectives that fail to challenge sexism and racism). Some questions I could have asked include: Why do we say that some interpretations are more correct than others? What lenses might some people have used to arrive at these interpretations? What results when we say that these interpretations are not only objective, but also the most correct? That is, whose lenses, experiences, perspectives, and questions get silenced, and whose interpretations become the norms or standards to which all other readers must conform? As a result, what social problems continue to go unnoticed?

Further reflection on my lesson reveals to me problems regarding the ways I asked students to make connections between the novel and their own lives. My questions often aimed to raise awareness of issues of race and racism, and in doing so, change how students thought about people whose racial identities differed from their own: How do your own life experiences help you to understand what the characters go through? How are you similar to and different from the characters? Such questions were certainly important for the ways they promoted empathy for social differences. However, such questions did not necessarily change how students thought about themselves.

In particular, such questions did not raise awareness of why students might have subconsciously desired thinking about social differences in only certain ways. After all, generally, students have already learned to make sense of the world through particular lenses, and they, often subconsciously, feel comfortable learning only things that map onto this worldview. That is, students often use lenses that reinforce the status quo. Thus, some questions I might also have asked include: What stereotypes did the students believe before reading the novel, and how did those stereotypes influence the ways that they read it? Were some stereotypes challenged, and were new ones created? Did the students pay attention to some things more than others? When were their expectations met or not met, and how did that make them feel about what they were reading? Why did they find certain characters or events more likable or believable than others? How do they understand the main points of the novel, and why? How does the novel complicate the ways they think about racial identity, discrimination, and race relations? What does the novel suggest that they themselves need to work on if they are to work toward social justice in their own lives? When learning about social differences through literature, it is important that students examine what they have already learned (and what they desire relearning) and the ways that such knowledge and desires affect how they read.

READING AGAINST RACISM

Teaching and learning against oppression requires asking different kinds of questions when reading literature. The "classics" are not inherently oppressive: They can be useful in an anti-oppressive lesson if teachers ask questions about the ways they reinforce the privilege of only certain experiences and perspectives. Conversely, "multicultural" literature is not inherently anti-oppressive: They can reinforce stereotypes if teachers fail to ask questions about how students are reading them. This is not to say that schools can continue to teach only the classics and just change the kinds of questions they ask, since the classics are limited in what they represent and how they represent it. Rather, this is to say that merely including multicultural literature without a change in how we read can be a problem.

As an illustration, consider the contentious debate over another novel that erupted a few years ago within a national association for Asian American studies. The committee responsible for awarding the outstanding work of fiction had selected a book that some in the association found offensive. The best-selling novel, written by a prominent Asian American author, featured Asian American characters growing up in Hawai'i whose experiences resonated with some readers. The committee argued that the book exemplified qualities that scholars of English literature have defined as the qualities of good literature. Critics argued that the book perpetuated stereotypes of certain Asian American ethnic groups that have traditionally been marginalized within Asian America, particularly Filipino Americans. Especially contentious, though often unspoken, was the sexual deviance attributed to one of the Filipino American characters. Although supporters of the committee insisted that a piece of literature that met the criteria of "outstanding" literature should not be disqualified for "political" reasons, critics insisted that any association trying to advance the welfare of Asian Americans should not be awarding a book that is politically harmful. They argued that awarding this book not only ignored the ways it perpetuated stereotypes, but also demonstrated that, yet again, certain ethnic groups did not matter as much as others within larger Asian America. In the end, the association voted to withdraw the award.

I remember feeling deeply concerned about the terms of this debate. The question of whether or not a book that meets the criteria for "outstanding" literature should be disqualified for "political" reasons is a question that assumes that the criteria are not already political. The debate, in other words, assumed that it was possible for a book to be "good" regardless of its political implications and that the decision of whether or not to praise the book depended only on whether the association valued aesthetics more than political correctness. What was not being debated was whether the criteria that literary scholars have traditionally used to determine the quality of literary works are themselves problematic. After all, such criteria have exalted as classics the very literature that we are saying is reinforcing the privilege of certain groups in society. We should not be surprised that such criteria overlook the oppressive tendencies of even "multicultural" literature.

The debate highlighted ways in which any piece of literature is necessarily partial. Any piece of literature can only include certain voices, experiences, and perspectives. Even lengthy texts that delve deeply into the complexities of human experience or the diversity of a community can tell us only so much about a person, or a group, or an event, or a culture. These partial stories cannot help but to challenge some stereotypes even while reinforcing others. The debate also highlighted ways in which any interpretation of literature is necessarily partial. Literature can mean (politically) different things to different people since we all read using lenses that have been colored by our unique identities and life experiences. Some readers might favor awarding the book because they have long struggled to include Asian American literature in the English canon, or because the book rings true to their experiences growing up in Hawai'i, or because they had just finished reading another of the author's books and couldn't wait to get ahold of this one. Other readers might challenge the award because they have long struggled to challenge the stereotypes and exclusion of Filipino Americans in Asian America, or because their experiences as disabled or gay/lesbian/bisexual/transgender or working-class Asian Americans help them to identify with these struggles from the margins. And still others might respond with ambivalence, given the contradictions in the debate regarding, say, sexual politics. What this means is, challenging oppression in the field of English literature needs to involve raising questions about the very ways we read.

For teachers of English literature, this debate within Asian American studies suggests that anti-oppressive education involves several things: It involves reading various literatures that tell a range of different stories. It involves examining how any piece of literature tells only certain stories and how different stories have different implications. It involves learning the literature and interpretations that matter in society. And it involves reflecting on how we as readers use different lenses to read and how those lenses make possible only certain understandings, emotions, and changes. What makes the field of English literature particularly well suited for anti-oppressive education is its insistence that we need to be changing not only what we read, but also how we read.

LOOKING BEYOND: LENSES OF TEACHERS

In my seminars with student teachers, I have always had classes that consisted primarily of White American students. In lessons on multi-culturalism and English literature, our discussions have invariably turned to their concerns regarding their abilities or inabilities to teach about racial differences and, perhaps more importantly, to teach across racial differences. Such concerns were especially the case for those students who planned to leave the very ivory tower in which they were being schooled to teach in more racially mixed settings. We would discuss the importance of acknowledging and interrupting their privileges as White Americans. We would discuss the importance of learning about and from their students so as to draw connections between literature and students' lives and to teach about the lenses students were using to read (and where those lenses may have come from). We would examine images in popular culture and in educational research of White English teachers crossing racial divides with their students of color. And we would conclude that, Yes, such teaching is possible.

But we would also discuss the aspects of students' life histories, emotions, identities, and prior knowledge that teachers may never be able to know, including aspects of which the students themselves are not consciously aware, and the ways such things can influence what and how students learn. We would discuss the dangers of presuming that we as teachers ever know "enough" about our students and do not have more homework to do, such as when we design a lesson for students whom we expect to be interested in certain things. We would discuss the unpredictable and evolving ways that racism and White-privilege play out in our daily lives, and the implication that, as White teachers, the work of interrupting one's own privileges is never done.

We would even discuss the problem of assuming that teachers of color are necessarily better able to connect with students of color (or White teachers with White students). It certainly helps to share certain histories or knowledge about one's local community, and the symbolic significance of shared identities should not be underestimated: In my own experiences, some of my teachers who shared certain of my identities gave me a sense of security or belonging that no conversation with other teachers afforded. But students are complex beings. An Asian American student has many other identities than that of Asian American, making it quite likely that even an Asian American teacher will fail to understand that student, including what would make that student engage with what it is that student is being taught. Furthermore, assumptions about what it means to "be" a certain identity often go hand-in-hand with assumptions that privilege other identities, as when being Asian American presumes being "normal" in other ways (heterosexual, able-bodied). Such conjoined identities make it quite likely that teachers who share the racial or cultural background of their students are making problematic and even faulty assumptions about those students, albeit unintentionally so.

My student teachers often expressed frustration over the contradictory implications of these theories and the notion that the work of interrupting our own privileges (racial, gender, or otherwise) and coming to know our students will never end. I would often agree that such insights certainly can make the process of teaching feel uncontrollable and impossible. Yet, I would also encourage my students to consider ways that the contradictions and ongoing work can present rich opportunities to challenge oppression in schools. Imagine if the incomplete knowledge we have of our students was a part of what gets discussed in the classroom. Imagine if the limits of our knowledge get discussed in ways that teach students about the partial nature of what and how they are learning. We might ask: Why did we do this lesson? What did this lesson assume students already knew or would be interested in? What social and cultural differences were being ignored in this lesson, and how did that influence who engaged and what was learned? Just as we work with students to examine their lenses for reading literature, so too should we work with students to examine the teachers' lenses for reading them. Although such an approach to teaching would require of teachers a level of vulnerability that we do not often expect in the classroom, perhaps it would also model for students what it means to look beyond the lesson.

QUESTIONS FOR REFLECTION AND DISCUSSION

1. (Comprehension) How can canonical literature be both oppressive and anti-oppressive? How can "multicultural" literature be both oppressive and anti-oppressive?
2. (Concretization) What are the different types of questions that readers can ask about a given text, and how might each type of question allow the reader to "see" different things?
3. (Critique) If you were involved in the debate over the Asian American fiction award, how would you have defined the criteria for the winning book?

SAMPLING OF NEW RESOURCES

For analyses of English and literacy education:

- Albright, J., & Luke, A. (Eds.). (2007). *Pierre Bourdieu and Literacy Education.* Mahwah, NJ: Lawrence Erlbaum.
- Blackburn, M. V., & Clark, C. T. (2007). *Literacy Research for Political Action and Social Change.* New York: Peter Lang.
- Greene, S. (2008). *Literacy as a Civil Right: Reclaiming Social Justice in Literacy Teaching and Learning.* New York: Peter Lang.
- Miller, S. J., Beliveau, L.B., Destigter, T., Kirland, D., & Rice, P. (2008). *Narratives of Social Justice Teaching: How English Teachers Negotiate Theory and Practice Between Preservice and Inservice Spaces.* New York: Peter Lang.

8

EXAMPLES FROM MUSIC

As MUSIC EDUCATION moves away from saying that "classical" music from Western Europe exemplifies the best that music has to offer, more and more teachers of music are also challenging the notions that there are correct ways of interpreting music and best ways of producing music. They are teaching students that interpreting music can involve searching for connections between the music and the context in which it was produced, such as its historical influences and the experiences or intent of the artist. It can involve reflecting on the various lenses being used by audiences to understand, evaluate, or emotionally respond to music. It can involve inquiring why some pieces or styles of music seem to matter more in society. Similarly, when teaching students to compose or perform, music teachers are teaching that producing music can involve experiencing how different formats allow musicians to express themselves in different ways, which in turn allows the audience to respond intellectually and emotionally in different ways.

All of these changes in music education help to explain why more and more teachers are making their curriculum "multicultural." They are including songs and genres from different cultures, discussing the personal backgrounds of artists who represent groups traditionally marginalized in society, and revealing some of the cultural influences on how different people interpret music. Such was my own approach to teaching music during a summer academic program for middle and high school students. For several weeks, I taught a singing class.

Toward the end of the program when students organized a talent show, the class formed a choir that performed several of the songs we studied. I had brought a wide variety of songs to class for the students to discuss and rehearse, including religious hymns, jazz songs, folk songs, songs from Broadway musicals, pop songs, and songs from cultures around the world. With most of the songs, our pre-rehearsal discussions were brief: We would discuss things like the genre, when and where it was written and by whom, and how people have responded differently to the songs. However, I expanded our discussions about some of the songs to include lessons about the songs' cultural contexts. These songs—folks songs from Japan and songs from early Hawai'i—provided an opportunity to share with the students some of my personal experiences in other cultures. What were the Japanese customs or foods or places to which the songs referred? What was it like for me to grow up in Hawai'i? I felt the music lessons were a great opportunity to teach students who, for the most part, were not of Japanese descent and had never been to Hawai'i, about social and cultural differences.

Years later, in a seminar for student teachers, I found myself again teaching one of those songs from Hawai'i. Students had just read about various approaches to multicultural education, and I was interested in exploring multiple multicultural approaches to teaching music. I was especially interested in exploring alternatives to the foods-and-festivals approach to multicultural education that I took during my summer stint. I am not suggesting that my summer students should not have learned about such differences. Our discussions about Japanese and Hawaiian cultures not only gave richer meaning to the songs we sang, but also expanded students' awareness of the world around them. However, I am suggesting that I needed to do more. Too often, we teach and learn about differences in ways that are simplistic and, therefore, comforting. So, with my student teachers, I wondered what it would mean to teach music in ways that get at complexity and critical awareness and that center on feelings of discomfort.

CHRISTIANITY, COLONIALISM, AND A SONG FROM HAWAI'I

I began my lesson on multicultural education by explaining that I wanted to focus the day's lesson on music. With many students watching me wide-eyed and smiling, I sang a musical scale (do-re-mi-fa-so-la-ti-do). I then described my interest in teaching a lesson that was out of the ordinary and that therefore required not only some risk-taking for both the students and me, but also some trust as we stepped outside of our comfort zones. Asking students to stand in a circle, I quickly shared tips on singing, and I conducted us through several warm-up scales.

I then told my students about my experiences singing in a choir when I was their age studying at a similarly small liberal arts college. Like many other college choirs, my choir sang many "classical" pieces, that is, songs from the Western European Christian tradition of music. One of my favorite pieces was a well-known Gregorian chant, "Kyrie Eleison," which for centuries people have used not only for religious worship, but also as the basis for creating other songs. Saying "la" in place of words, I first taught them the melody of the beginning of the chant. After learning the pronunciation of the lyrics in Latin, we sang the first few lines. We then discussed stereotypical images that came to mind when we heard the words "Christianity" or "Christian music." Students brainstormed: large stone cathedrals, the holy cross, the Bible, stained-glass windows, pipe organs, church choirs wearing long robes, televangelists, ministers preaching, pews, people praying silently, people singing loudly. Acknowledging that these images were indeed a part of the histories and cultures of Christianity, I asked students to close their eyes and picture these images while I sang the entire chant. I asked them to reflect on the meanings and feelings that arose when they juxtaposed these images with the song.

Jumping ahead almost one thousand years and halfway around the world, I continued the lesson by telling my students about my experiences growing up in Hawai'i. Like many other elementary schools in the United States, mine spent time each week studying music, sometimes by playing the recorder, but usually by singing different songs. We sang children's songs, folk songs from early U.S. history, and holiday songs around Christmas. Unlike most places in the United States, however, we also studied music quite unique to Hawai'i: We practiced strumming the ukulele, and we sang a number of Hawaiian songs. My favorite Hawaiian song, "Kanaka Waiwai," was one that I probably learned around fourth grade. Its lyrics were first written over a century ago, and it is a popular song even today in Hawai'i.

As before, we learned the song by first singing "la" to the opening tunes, then pronouncing the Hawaiian lyrics, and finally, singing the beginning of the song. And, as before, we discussed the stereotypical images that came to mind when we heard the words "Hawai'i," "Hawaiian music," and "Hawaiian culture." Students generated a similarly long list: coconut trees, Waikiki, *Baywatch* (the TV show), beaches, tanned bodies, men on surfboards, women in *mu'umu'us* (dresses), hula dancers with grass skirts, ukuleles, *luaus* (outdoor feasts), *poi* (pounded taro root), flower leis, volcanoes. Acknowledging that these images were indeed a part of the histories and cultures of Hawai'i, and that these images were likely the ones taught in brief lessons about Hawai'i (especially if teachers have only a brief period to give a cultural context to whatever song or text they are teaching), I asked students to close their eyes and picture these images as I sang the first half of the song. I again asked them to reflect on the meanings and feelings that arose when they juxtaposed these images with the song.

Asking the students to open their eyes, I proceeded to tell a different story about Hawai'i, one that was not often heard. Hawai'i is the only state in the United States to have been ruled by a monarchy. Each of the islands in the Hawaiian chain used to be ruled by different chiefs, until the beginning of the nineteenth century when one of these chiefs—Kamehameha I—united the islands into one kingdom. For almost one hundred years, the kingdom was ruled by King Kamehameha and, in turn, seven of his descendants: four other Kamehamehas, King Lunalilo, King Kalakaua, and Queen Lili'uokalani. Toward the end of the nineteenth century, Queen Lili'uokalani was forced to abdicate her throne, and a few years later Hawai'i became a territory of the United States. Of course, many factors contributed to the overthrow of the monarchy. Former kings had gradually lost power to a constitutional government in response to weighty opposition to monarchical rule, especially among wealthy settlers from the United States. And, although the U.S. government determined that the overthrow was unlawful, it did not help to reinstate the monarchy. Instead, it acquired Hawai'i as a territory just a few years later, which was timely, given that the United States was just entering the Spanish-American War and needed a Pacific base.

Significant for my lesson, however, was the information that businessmen and political leaders from abroad were not the only ones who made possible the overthrow of the monarchy and the acquisition of Hawai'i by the United States. Also involved were Christian missionaries. Early on, they worked to change Hawai'i into a place that belonged in the more "civilized" and "moral" world of the Protestant United States. As advocates for U.S. acquisition, they were among those who worked to lessen the powers of earlier kings, especially regarding perspectives and practices regarding land ownership and wealth, and who directly confronted the queen and forced her to abdicate. This should not be surprising. The goal of missionaries is often to help "them" be more like "us," and in this case, to educate Hawaiians in the ways that "Americans" are educated and to get Hawaiians to worship in the ways that Protestant Americans worship. Indeed, from early in the Kamehameha dynasty, missionaries began extensive outreach that gradually gained more influence over the native people of Hawai'i. And their impact was substantial: Churches sprang up, and native religion faded as even the monarchs began officially supporting missionary efforts and beliefs. Elements of "traditional" Hawaiian culture, including the themes of more and more songs and dances, began centering on Christianity, and today Christianity continues to impact Hawai'i in ways that change the cultures of Native Hawaiians.

I told my students that it was not until well beyond my elementary school years that I noticed that the lyrics of my favorite Hawaiian song centered on a Christian theme. Although I had learned the song from a handout with the English translation printed on it, I do not remember looking carefully at the translation, or perhaps I did but did not feel it was strange for the story being told to be a Christian one. I passed out the lyrics to my students, and as I read aloud through the Hawaiian text, students read the English translation. The song is a parable from the New Testament. The parable tells of Jesus who meets a wealthy man. When the man asks Jesus what he must do to have eternal life, Jesus tells him to give away his possessions. The song does not go on to say how Jesus explained the importance of giving away possessions for getting into Heaven, perhaps because those hearing the song are expected to know the full parable already.

In light of this discussion, I explained to my students that there are many ways to tell a story about a culture. Some stories can repeat the stereotypical knowledge that, while in some ways true, is certainly not all there is to know about that culture. Such stories may be easy to tell because they conform to what people already know or have experienced, or because they present a clear and simple picture that makes coming to "understand" that culture easy and doable. Other stories can paint very different pictures, ones that challenge the ways we already think about a culture. Stories such as the one about the overthrow of the Hawaiian monarchy can tell us not only that a culture is much more complex than we traditionally think, but also that the ways we traditionally think can be very problematic. It is problematic, for instance, to think of Hawai'i as a tropical paradise full of fun and fantasy when there is a history of domination and racism against which people have long struggled and continue to struggle. In modern-day Hawai'i, the U.S. military, media, capitalist industries, and tourists continue to impose significantly on life in Hawai'i, and even those of us who are not native Hawaiians but consider Hawai'i our home do not often acknowledge, much less challenge, this cultural imperialism. Thinking of Hawai'i as a tourist getaway assumes that Hawai'i is something for "us" to consume and, in turn, makes it difficult for people to acknowledge how "we" contribute to problems in Hawai'i.

I suggested to my students that perhaps there is a reason why we often tell only certain stories about Hawai'i. Perhaps telling only simplistic, stereotypical stories allows us to continue ignoring how the majority in the United States have acted and continue to act in colonialist ways toward the people, lands, and cultures of Hawai'i. Similarly, perhaps there is a reason why we often tell only certain stories about Christianity. Perhaps thinking about Christianity in terms of the helpful things it brings into our lives (faith, worship, community, beauty, peace) allows us to ignore the ways that certain Christian institutions or groups of people can bring harm into our lives. In fact, even when the stories we tell are of the visible and contentious ways that certain Christian institutions have been harmful—for example, by opposing rights of women over their own bodies and of all people over their own sexual activities—we often continue to ignore the less visible and less contentious ways that Christianity affects society or, in this case, Hawai'i.

I concluded the lesson by asking students to close their eyes once again as they pictured the images of Hawai'i suggested by my retelling of Hawaiian history and culture. I sang the entire song. And, as before, I asked them to consider the meanings and feelings that arose when they juxtaposed these images with the song.

As the students opened their eyes, I asked them to reflect on this lesson. They debated the ways that the song could "mean" different things: a sign that Christianity has "taken over" Hawai'i, a sign that Christianity has appropriated Hawaiian language and culture, a sign that, rightly or wrongly, some in Hawai'i follow Christianity. Students described ways that different moments in the lesson invited different feelings for the same song: peaceful at one moment, angry at another; spiritually uplifted at one moment, sad at another; entertained at one moment, deceived at another. Perhaps more important, students described how certain cultural images made them feel like they "understood" the correct meaning of the song, whereas other images made them feel as though the meaning of the song depended on many factors and that they therefore felt a desire to learn more about such factors (including the histories of Hawai'i that are silenced and why this silence exists). Students described, in other words, how it is possible to design lessons that challenge oppression by showing not only that there are multiple ways of "understanding," but also that there is much more to know and that what we already know is problematic. Even the student who said he did not feel there was any difference between the two versions of the song invited discussion about the importance of acknowledging the different ways that students might respond, and the possibility that students will respond in ways entirely unexpected by the teacher.

LOOKING BEYOND: RISKS AND EMOTIONS

Emotions played a big role in this lesson. This is not surprising, given that music education and arts education in general are premised, in part, on the importance of learning to express oneself and to experience life through our various senses, including our senses of sound and rhythm and melody and harmony. Why are such expressions and experiences important? Because they can invoke memories and images and ideas and, of course, emotions in ways that prose or conversation cannot. Toward this end, I asked students to take the risk of stepping out of their comfort zones and engaging in an activity that was not traditionally considered an academic lesson. I asked students to picture certain images, listen to a song, and reflect on what the combination of the images and song meant and felt to them. I asked students to compare and contrast their emotional reactions, and then examine the insights into multicultural education made possible when their emotions matter in a lesson. And at the end of the lesson students were not left with a reassuring "answer" to the problem of how to teach in a multicultural way. Rather, they were left with contradictory notions of how different pedagogical contexts make possible different ways to make sense of cultural texts. If anything, they were left with an explicitly partial "answer" that raised many more questions and perhaps reminded them that anti-oppressive education can be a pretty uncomfortable process.

When I concluded the class period, I asked students to share possible reasons why we as teachers might be concerned about teaching a lesson like this. Though creative and interactive, this lesson certainly could operate in contradictory ways. My students suggested that the lesson, while aiming to invite forms of discomfort that fostered students' learning, was likely inviting other forms of discomfort that inhibited some students from learning. Not all students would feel comfortable singing, especially in a class where they were not among close friends. Not all students would feel comfortable (and might even feel offended) being forced to sing a song about Jesus, especially if they were not Christian. Not all students would feel comfortable learning about an oppressive history of missionaries, especially if they were scheduled to participate in a religious outreach program during the upcoming summer in a "third world" country. Not all students would feel comfortable learning about problems of the tourist industry, especially if they had recently returned from a vacation in a place like Hawai'i. Not all students would be physically capable of standing for long periods of time. There exist a range of ways in which students can feel uncomfortable—emotionally, physically. My students suggested that, as teachers, they would need to be able to address these forms of discomfort, not by ridding the classroom of them, but by making them somehow an acknowledged part of the lesson. Failing to address these forms of discomfort, after all, will likely constitute a hidden message that works against their anti-oppressive goals.

Hidden messages certainly permeated my teaching, and as I expected, our discussion of the strengths and weaknesses of my lesson did lead me into my own little crisis when one of my students suggested a possible hidden message that contradicted my goals. The student noticed that, during the warm-up activity, I instructed students to breathe in certain ways, to form their mouths in certain ways, even to position their bodies in certain ways. What I had learned and was now teaching to be the "correct" way to use the body to produce music was, of course, one of many ways of singing, and ironically, a way of singing that had been privileged in the tradition of music that I just critiqued as dominating music education in U.S. schools. I humbly admitted that, Yes, it is indeed ironic that my lesson on the colonialist nature of what we want students to sing and what we tell students about music's cultural context can simultaneously reinforce the colonialist nature of *how* we want students to sing. And this is exactly my point—that such contradictions can always be found. And while some teachers might despair at the impossibility of seamless lessons, I encouraged my students—and, I hope, demonstrated through my own response—to think of these contradictions as the very things that, when discussed, can help their students to "look beyond" the lessons and learn in anti-oppressive ways. In fact, perhaps it is in moments like this, when students exceed my expectations, that anti-oppressive learning is really happening. Perhaps it would have been a problem if students did not learn to raise critical questions about how I was teaching music, or how

I was teaching about Hawaii, or how I expected only certain responses from them. And in fact, is that not how some critics have characterized multicultural education, namely, as replacing one (socially dominant) view of the world with another (politically correct) one, even though neither view can help but be partial? Such discussions certainly made clear to me that what can make the field of music especially well suited for anti-oppressive education is its ability to reveal hidden ways that oppression regulates not only what we think, but also how we feel and express those feelings. These hidden messages need to be examined in the classroom.

QUESTIONS FOR REFLECTION AND DISCUSSION

1. (Comprehension) What are aspects of music—from its cultural context and lyrical content to performance expectations and consumer desires—that can privilege certain cultures, groups, and identities over others? What are aspects of other art forms (visual arts, theater, dance, etc.) that can privilege certain cultures, groups, and identities?
2. (Concretization) How might you design a lesson about a song that engages students in critical analysis of the various aspects noted in Question #1?
3. (Critique) What are other risks involved when teaching and learning in ways that call explicitly on our emotions, bodies, artistic imaginations, and desires, and how might these be addressed productively in a classroom?

SAMPLING OF NEW RESOURCES

For analyses of music and arts education:

- Lea, V., & Sims, E. J. (Eds.). (2008). *Undoing Whiteness in the Classroom: Critical Educultural Teaching Approaches for Social Justice Activism.* New York: Peter Lang.
- Volk, T. M. (2004). *Music, Education, and Multiculturalism: Foundations and Principles.* Oxford: Oxford University Press.
- Woodford, P. G. (2005). *Democracy and Music Education: Liberalism, Ethics, and the Politics of Practice.* Bloomington, IN: Indiana University Press.

9

EXAMPLES FROM "FOREIGN" LANGUAGES

Many people seem to consider the study of "foreign" or nonnative languages to be a discipline that is especially well positioned to address issues of social and cultural differences. For students whose native language is English, it teaches how to communicate with different cultural and linguistic groups in the United States and throughout the world. For students who are learning to speak English, it teaches how to communicate in the dominant language in U.S. society and, therefore, gives access to privileges that come with speaking English. For all students, it teaches about different groups of people, the cultures in which different languages operate, and the cultural assumptions that frame how the languages are used. Some might argue that lessons about cultural differences can detract from the primary goal of learning a different language, but to many language teachers, the notion that learning a language goes hand-in-hand with learning about a culture just makes common sense.

Such was my own approach to teaching language/culture. I once taught a series of lessons on Nepali language to high school students. Some of my lessons on language invited related lessons on culture. For instance, teaching my students some of the Nepali words for "school," "math," "student," and "toilet" provided ample opportunities for me to describe my observations from living in Nepal on what schools looked like, what textbooks consisted of, how students were treated, and what sanitation was like. Some of my language lessons even *required* that students learn the cultural context of language. I remember explaining that, in the village where I lived (and in many places throughout Nepal), "rice" also meant "meal," which made sense given that people in the village generally ate two meals a day, make up almost always of lentil soup and lots of rice. The poverty of the village helped to explain the thinness of the people, which is why "how fat!" (instead of "you're so thin") was a compliment and why "have you eaten?" (instead of "how are you?" or "what's up?") was a common greeting.

Knowing cultural norms was necessary to prevent miscommunication, especially given that norms of communicating in one cultural setting are not necessarily norms in other settings. For instance, it took me a while to realize that people in my village did not generally answer questions with a "yes." Rather, they either tilted their head to the side (which I had interpreted as "I don't care" or "whatever" while in the United States) or repeated the key word of the question (as by answering "school" if I asked, "are you going to school now?"). So, in response to "Have you eaten?" I learned to tilt my head and respond to someone's greeting with, "I've eaten."

I had first realized the importance of understanding the cultural context of language usage a few years earlier when living in Nepal and teaching English-as-a-second-language to elementary and middle schoolers. In my ESL classes, I found myself making constant reference to life in the United States when trying to explain why we could not simply translate into English what was otherwise appropriate in Nepal. We would look at pictures or articles from magazines, and we would role-play scenarios where people were greeting one another, eating a meal, or purchasing an item. All along, I would point to similarities and differences between what was often taken-for-granted in Nepal and what was often taken-for-granted in the United States during everyday conversations.

Just as my students would point out that there is great diversity among the people of Nepal, so too would I point out that there is great diversity among the people of the United States. I especially appreciated these opportunities to teach about the diversity in the United States, given the stereotypes and generalizations I often confronted from students and adults alike about the United States. I would explain that, in contrast to images in popular culture or reports from the media, there are many "Americans" (myself included) who are not White, are not wealthy, do not live in places that snow, are not Christian, and do not support everything the U.S. government does around the world. Teaching English gave me opportunities not only to teach about a different society, but also to challenge prevailing ideas about such differences.

As is true of more and more language teachers, I have come to view "foreign" language classrooms as ideal places to learn about social differences in ways that challenge students' lack of knowledge and/or misknowledge of people who are different from them. Teaching about differences is especially important when many of the groups about whom students are learning are the groups labeled "minorities" in the United States. Spanish-language classrooms can teach about the cultures of various Latino/a, Chicano/a, Mexicano/a, and Puerto Ricano/a communities; Chinese-language classrooms can teach about the cultures of various Chinese American ethnic communities; sign-language classrooms can teach about the cultures of various deaf communities. And they can do so in ways that challenge both stereotypes and the notion that these "minority" cultures and communities are somehow less important, less valuable, less "normal," or otherwise less than the majority or dominant group of society.

CULTURAL CONTEXT AND THE PROBLEM OF DIFFERENCE

I have also come to believe that teaching about differences can be a very contradictory process. I have two concerns. First, teaching about differences can reinforce stereotypes. When I think about what I told my high school students about Nepal, I am struck by the simplicity of my portrayal. I told my students that Nepal and Nepali people are *like this*. True, my goal was merely to provide some context in which the language we were learning made sense, and thus, I chose not to devote much time to portray Nepal in much depth and chose instead to simplify or simply ignore much of the complexities of Nepali cultures. Such simplification always happens when we try to teach about a culture: We include only certain aspects and present these aspects in a manageable lesson. Unfortunately, by simplifying things so that the lesson "makes sense," we end up telling a partial story (consisting of only some of what is and can be known about Nepal) that often gets generalized for all of Nepal. Students can end up believing that they now understand Nepali cultures and peoples: "real" Nepali customs look like this, "authentic" Nepali food tastes like this, all Nepali students act like this. Students can end up thinking about Nepal through stereotypes, which was exactly what my lesson on Nepal was trying to change.

What is the alternative? Although it is important to include a range of materials in order to enrich students' understanding of Nepal, it is also important to recognize that our teaching can never be fully inclusive. Geography, gender, political perspectives, educational background, ethnic heritage, religion, and countless other social markers can distinguish one cultural group or individual experience from another, and cultures and communities themselves are constantly changing as people grapple with different ideas, interact with different groups, and incorporate different customs and values and lifestyles. The solution is not merely to tell a "fuller" story since the problem is not merely that the story is partial. The problem is that we do not often make this partialness explicit and challenge the ways that the story—even a diverse one—can become a stereotype. It does not take much time to teach students to look critically at the story being told about Nepal.

If given the chance to go back in time and reteach the lessons on Nepali language, I can imagine revising the lessons in several ways. I can imagine adding information about cultural contexts in which language takes on different meanings. I might ask, How do gender, socioeconomic status, and educational background matter when people are greeting one another? As the "American" teacher who was male and comparatively wealthy, my experiences with greetings were quite specific to my identities. People were not all greeted equally, and as I reflect back, I can remember younger women teachers greeting me and the older Nepali male teachers quite differently than they were greeted in return. By including such information, I can ask students to reflect not only on social hierarchies in Nepal, but also on how silencing these dynamics in my lesson could have taught that "real" Nepali culture and language are those associated with the privileged in society (i.e., those who are male, wealthy, and educated).

When revising the lesson, I can also imagine adding information about historical influences on culture and language. I might ask, How has Western colonialism affected the ways Nepalis talk about schooling? We can see a long history of British colonialism in neighboring South Asian countries, especially India, as well as a more recent history of U.S. influence in the form of aid (including Peace Corps volunteers) in Nepal. These histories have influenced not only the structure of schooling (with curriculum divided into disciplines, students promoted by standardized and high-stakes tests) but also the perception of what schools are supposed to look like. By including such information, I can ask students to reflect not only on colonialism in Nepal, but also on how silencing these histories in my lesson could have taught that the United States has only played helpful roles in changing Nepal schools.

These lessons on the diversity or historical changes within cultures could make difficult any attempt to give a clear context for the language being learned. After all, it is difficult to say that language takes on a particular meaning in a particular context when it is unclear exactly what that context is. And perhaps this difficulty arises from viewing both language and culture as fixed entities. But what if, just as we view culture, we view language as something that is constantly evolving, necessarily contradictory and contested, and used in different ways by different groups of people in different contexts. There are many variations, for example, within the Nepali language. The version taught in schools or taught to those like me who are privileged by gender, class, and educational background may not reflect the versions that exist among other groups or that are being developed by those on the margins of society, including certain ethnic, gender, and religious groups. This variation even exists within the English language used here in the United States: Some versions have a notable accent (Midwestern versus Southern), some versions use words differently ("soda" versus "pop"), some versions blend in words from other languages (as with Hawai'i creole English, i.e., "pidgin" English), and some versions carry different social values ("standard" English versus "street talk"). Why is this significant? As with lessons on the "true" culture, lessons that claim to teach the "authentic" language cannot help but maintain the privilege of only certain groups in society while erasing the differences of other groups. Lessons on language need to expose the differences within any community and the reasons why those differences have been, until now, silenced in schools. We might ask, Why do we often teach only certain aspects of a language but classify those aspects as the "authentic" language of a group? It may be simpler to ignore the ongoing tensions in a community and variations in a language, and yet, those complexities may be exactly what are needed to teach a language in anti-oppressive ways.

My second concern when teaching about differences is the focus on the "Other," on whatever or whoever is "different." Teaching about differences can further objectify the Other. As teachers, we often believe that learning about different cultures or groups of people is important for at least two reasons. Learning about differences can help students appreciate differences, as when realizing that there is beauty or value in cultures and experiences that are different from our own, such as the different foods people eat, the holidays they celebrate, and the customs they practice. Learning about differences can also help students recognize similarities and realize that others are not much different from themselves—we all feel pain, form loving relationships, and help others in need. Whether seeing others as different from me or similar to me, the goal seems to be the same: to change how I see and feel about others. In fact, common sense often tells us that oppression results from misinformed views of others and that if we can just learn more about one another, humanize one another, and see how we are similar while appreciating how we are unique, then our problems will be solved.

Significant, here, is the recognition that learning about differences is often something we feel comfortable, and even desire, doing, perhaps because it allows us to continue to focus our gaze on "them" and not really change how we think about "us." For example, my own experiences suggest that it is easier to learn about a culture when that culture is understood as something foreign to me, that is, separate from my normal life. Their foreignness is what can make other cultures seem entertaining, exciting, mysterious, exotic, even erotic, which are some of the very reasons that people travel as tourists to different countries, study abroad, or collect artifacts and even spouses from other places. Although certainly not always the case, it does seem to be quite common for the foreignness of others, of "those people," to capture our attention. We often want to see, collect, or learn about that which is different from ourselves.

Fortunately, lessons about other cultures do not have to teach only about the Other. It can also teach us about ourselves. Learning about how people in Nepal tend to talk about food can raise questions about how I talk about food and why I tend to find alternative ways of talking about food strange. It might lead me to ask, What meanings do I normally attribute to foods and eating? What do I normally define as "snacks," "breakfast," "healthy," "kids' foods," or foods that "fit" a party, a romantic dinner, or a business luncheon? Learning about how people in Nepal tend to talk about school holidays, or important figures in history, or romance can raise questions about how I talk about such things and why I have come to believe that my ways are the most sensible, valuable, important, or correct. Why do we take a holiday for this historical figure but not that one? Why do we think marriage is supposed to look like this but not like that? And why do I often think it is weird when someone thinks otherwise? Learning about how people in Nepal tend to talk about education can raise questions about how I talk about education and about the reasons why only certain approaches to education seem to make sense to me. It might lead me to ask, What approaches to teaching and learning strike me as common sense? Why are "foreign"-language classes often electives, what versions of a language often get assessed on standardized exams, why does bilingual education frequently aim only to mainstream the ESL students as quickly as possible (rather than develop competence in two languages or cultures), and why are ESL students often separated from other students for so much of the school day?

Learning about how people in Nepal tend to talk and the cultural assumptions and norms behind their language can raise questions about the often unspoken cultural assumptions and norms behind my own language and ideas. Every instance of challenging stereotypes about those who are different is an opportunity to examine parallel assumptions about those who are normal. Perhaps more important, such a turn inward can raise questions about why I value this norm and devalue whatever ideas, practices, or identities do not conform. Learning about other cultures can challenge my ideas about cultural normalcy and my investment in such ideas. So, yes, teaching "foreign" languages in anti-oppressive ways does involve changing our ideas about and relationships with others. But it also involves changing our ideas and feelings about ourselves.

LOOKING BEYOND: CULTURAL NORMS IN SCHOOLS

The field of "foreign" languages is uniquely positioned to teach students that we always think within a cultural context and, therefore, that our knowledge, values, identities, and perspectives are always framed by the languages we use and the cultures that situate those languages. Having grown up speaking a certain language within a certain culture, we are all necessarily limited in our abilities to make sense of this world. A significant reason, then, why learning "foreign" languages is important is that it can open up whole new ways of thinking. This opportunity does not only apply to advanced students who are capable of reading literatures and theories written in another language. The examples discussed throughout this chapter point to instances when learning about cultural contexts can invite questions about alternative ways of thinking about normalcy with the most novice of students.

Even teachers need to be open to raising questions about the limits of their knowledge and their assumptions about what is normal. In fact, sometimes when teachers raise questions about their own cultural assumptions, they can model the kind of self-critique and vulnerability that they invite their students to experience. Teachers could show that even they have work to do when challenging the norms that govern our lives. For example, when teaching about meals in Nepal, I might mention the "national meal" in Nepal and contrast that with how I think about meals in the United States. But there are many things my students might ask about my own views of what is normal concerning my meals: Did I notice that I described my meals in terms of the time of the day, being vegetarian or not, and a certain number of courses? Did I notice that I adopted what nutritionists call a balanced diet or a diet appropriate for a young, slim, healthy man? Did I notice that I did not mention any reliance on the food-service industry or any knowledge of how food production and consumption have been heavily regulated by commercial interests (farming industries, health-supplement industries)?

The fact that teachers will always think in ways that are already framed by their language and cultural assumptions might feel disconcerting to teachers. However, I suggest that such limitations in their knowledge can be exactly what will help their students to see the importance of looking beyond what any of us take for granted as they explore new possibilities for making sense of and living in this world.

QUESTIONS FOR REFLECTION AND DISCUSSION

1. (Comprehension) Why are "foreign" and "minority" in quotation marks, that is, how are these terms problematic?
2. (Comprehension) What is the relationship between teaching a language and teaching about a culture? What is the relationship between cultural norms and language norms?
3. (Concretization) How might you teach about a culture in ways that problematize cultural norms and cultural stereotypes?
4. (Critique) How might you teach about our own cultures in ways that problematize norms and "common sense?"

SAMPLING OF NEW RESOURCES

For analyses of "foreign" language education:

- Carpenter, V. M., Jesson, J., Roberts, P., & Stephenson, M. (Eds.). (2008). *Nga Kaupapa Here: Connections and Contradictions in Education*. South Melbourne, New Zealand: Cengage Learning.
- Kumaravadivelu, B. (2007). *Cultural Globalization and Language Education*. New Haven, CT: Yale University Press.
- Norton, B., & Toohey, K. (Eds.). (2004). *Critical Pedagogies and Language Learning*. Cambridge: Cambridge University Press.
- Osborn, T. A. (2005). *Teaching World Languages for Social Justice: A Sourcebook of Principles and Practices*. Mahwah, NJ: Lawrence Erlbaum.

10

EXAMPLES FROM THE NATURAL SCIENCES

I ONCE TAUGHT A SCIENCE LESSON to elementary students about water. I chose the topics I wanted them to learn, including what forms (solid, gaseous) water takes at different temperatures, why water boils or evaporates, and how we use water in our everyday lives. I chose the format for the lesson: Several students would work with me outside of class to prepare skits to illustrate these different topics, and then, in an interactive presentation, we would teach these topics. I made cardboard costumes to be tied onto students with string that represented water drops, the sun, a stove, a shirt hanging on a clothesline, a freezer. Dressed in these costumes, the students would accompany my presentation with short skits in which water drops hug when cold, wander away when caught in a sunny breeze, or run around when hot. In short, I framed my presentation of water with metaphors of human behavior.

My choices had strengths and weaknesses. In some ways, it was helpful to personify water. Students could relate what they were learning to something already familiar to them, such as hugging or running around. And, indeed, some properties of water do parallel human behaviors. However, as with any metaphor, the metaphor of human behavior does not capture all the qualities of water, and so a lesson based on these parallels oversimplifies how we understand water and even attributes qualities to water that do not really exist. For example, what influences human behavior are not only environmental factors but also our emotions.

This is not to say that I should have chosen a "better" metaphor for or way to think about water. Rather, it is to say that, like any other understanding of water, this understanding is helpful in some ways and not helpful in others. This is also not to say that I should have taught about water without any metaphor or story to frame my presentation of water. Arguably, there is nothing in the natural sciences that we understand outside of some underlying story, whether that story be a scientific theory, a cultural myth, a philosophical or religious perspective, or simply a lens that has been colored by our life experiences. This is why we often disagree about what a sign means or what an object is worth or what behavior is normal or what interpretation is correct: We rely on different stories to frame our understanding of the world. The "objective" or "commonsensical" understanding of the world is not a neutral one, but one that uses an unacknowledged, favored story.

It is important, then, that students learn that we are using different stories to understand the world, that different stories have different political implications, and that the stories currently framing the natural sciences do indeed have oppressive implications for U.S. society. In a seminar for student teachers, I once taught a lesson on different ways we could teach the same topic (namely, human reproduction), examining, for each approach, possible underlying stories and their different political implications.

GENDERED STORIES

I began the lesson by asking students to imagine that they were in a middle school life-sciences class and that the lesson took place at the end of our unit on human reproduction. Our assignment was, in small groups, to take a large piece of poster paper and draw a flowchart depicting how a fertilized egg can develop into a male and a female birth. Groups generally drew the same thing: A sperm fertilizes an egg; the fertilized egg undergoes cell division and reproduction; an embryo develops, as does its sex organs, which distinguish it as male or female; the gendered fetus grows larger and more complex; and at nine months, the baby is born. As we discussed our flowcharts, I asked students whether these drawings generally reflected what they remember learning in school. The consensus was, Yes.

I then asked students whether the way I framed the assignment made it easy to ignore other aspects of human reproduction. Some pointed to ways that the beginning of the flowchart fails to expose students to methods of fertilization other than heterosexual intercourse, as with fertilization in labs, surrogate parenting, and cloning. Some pointed to ways that the flowchart ignored interactions between the developing organism and the mother's womb, and ways that the end of the flowchart ignored the process of childbirth. Some pointed to ways that my asking students to show how the fertilized egg develops into a male and a female ignored ways that humans can develop with ambiguous genders. They noted that not all humans are clearly "male" or "female."

We do not often hear of these intersexed births. An estimated one in two thousand births has ambiguous genitalia and/or sex organs, as when some combination of "male" organs and "female" organs, sometimes fully developed, sometimes not, is present. More significantly, an estimated 1 to 4 percent of births have ambiguous chromosomes: Some combinations are neither XX (female) nor XY (male), but XO, for instance, or XXX or XXY. Yet we expect all humans to fit into one of two categories. We have two options for "sex" on birth certificates. We have two options for clothing and birth announcements in stores. We almost always ask, "Girl or boy?" when we hear of a newborn. When genitalia are ambiguous, we often surgically "correct" this ambiguity, even if it poses no health risks. Some children are unaware of their own intersexuality. Some parents are unaware that a surgical correction has occurred. Whether or not surgery takes place, parents often choose a particular gender and raise the child as that gender, perhaps because otherwise they realize their child will likely face significant harassment and distress, or perhaps because they believe their child is supposed to be one or the other.

I asked students to revisit their flowcharts and to add this new information. Groups generally added a third sequence (the dotted lines in Figure 3) to suggest that humans can develop as female, as male, or as intersexed. Some groups illustrated how, after birth, the intersexed baby is sometimes "fixed."

After sharing the revised drawings, I asked my students why we do not often learn about intersexuality, and, for that matter, why society seems to want to silence its occurrence. Some students suggested that, because much of the way society operates presumes that there are only two genders, it is simply more comfortable to continue operating as such rather than change, say, our restrooms, our laws, our ideas of romance, and our clothes. Some students suggested that certain privileges come with the notion that there are only two, inherently different genders. To say that there is a continuum of possible genders, or at least that it is possible for gender to be ambiguous, makes it difficult to

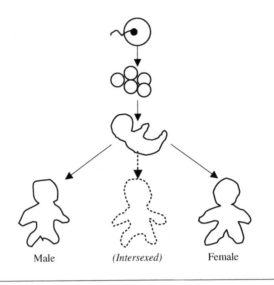

Male   (Intersexed)   Female

Fig. 3

assert that this is what women (or men) are like, are better at, or are supposed to do. Similarly, to say that there are more than two genders makes it difficult to assert that we are supposed to be sexually attracted only to members of the "opposite gender." What does it mean to be heterosexual or even bisexual when there are more than two genders? When we acknowledge intersexuality, we are forced to question the commonsensical ways that we think about gender norms, gender hierarchies, and sexual orientation. Building on this idea, some students also suggested that the ways we think about ourselves are often rooted in the idea that there are only two sexes. Acknowledging intersexuality forces us to confront the socially/medically/politically constructed nature of our own gender identities and sexual orientations, which is a process too uncomfortable for some people to undertake.

By excluding such topics as intersexuality, science curriculums reinforce a gendered status quo of society. However, I urged my students to resist concluding that, by including intersexuality, the curriculum would become complete or would no longer contribute to gender oppression. Many aspects of human reproduction remain excluded from the curriculum, including aspects we have yet to discover, and even if we could include everything, the curriculum cannot help but tell an underlying story about gender. In fact, I pointed out that in our flowcharts, the inclusion of intersexuality did not necessarily change an underlying story that reinforced gender norms.

Referring back to the flowcharts, I described other similarities I heard in their descriptions of human reproduction. Many sperm from the male enter the uterus, but only one, a very "active" one, "penetrates" the egg from the female and fertilizes it. In their first stages of development, embryos are "female" (or at least are more female-like), not sexually neutral. As they continue to grow, some embryos have sex organs that "remain" female. But some embryos have chromosomes that prompt their organs to "develop" into male organs by descending, elongating, closing. Babies born intersexed and surgically corrected will more likely be made female than male because it is "easier" to construct female genitalia.

Such a framing is not inaccurate. Sperms do fertilize eggs; early embryos do begin with female-like sex organs; males do develop different kinds of genitalia and organs than do females; intersexed babies are made to appear female more often than male. However, the language or images we use often reflect commonsensical, sexist assumptions about gender and gender relations: Maleness is active (penetrates, changes), femaleness is passive (is there to be penetrated, is what results if no changes are made). Maleness is more developed or somehow beyond femaleness, which is where both males and females "start," or which is easier to construct in terms of appearance and function. By thinking within this framework, we are already assuming that males are not just different but better than females.

Such assumptions about maleness and femaleness parallel the assumptions we often make about masculinity and femininity. Among men, masculinity is often something that needs to be constantly proven. To be considered masculine, men often feel they need to demonstrate their virility, athleticism, aggression, or stoicism. By doing so, they are showing that they are not passive, or weak, or emotional, or other things that men are not supposed to be. Proving that they are masculine, in other words, is a way of proving that they are not feminine, which is what they are labeled if they fail to prove otherwise. Thus, being feminine, as with being female, is where we naturally begin and where we develop from. At least, those are often the unspoken assumptions in society regarding gender.

This binary, hierarchical story is not the only way to understand gender, and throughout history, other cultures in this world have indeed understood gender in different ways. But in contemporary U.S. society and in our science curriculum, this binary story often goes unquestioned. As I concluded the lesson, I suggested that teaching science in anti-oppressive ways requires not merely including a wider range of topics and perspectives. Inclusion is certainly important, especially when it reveals the existence and value of all kinds of differences in the natural world. But regardless of what is included, students need to examine the underlying stories of the curriculum and the ways that the stories can both reinforce and challenge oppression.

LOOKING BEYOND: STORIES ABOUT SCIENCE

The emphasis in the natural sciences on producing knowledge about the natural world in a systematic, verifiable way (using the "scientific method") often implies that its process of producing knowledge is objective or bias-free. When combined with an analysis of the science curriculum's underlying stories and their complicity with oppression, this emphasis is exactly what can help to make the natural sciences especially well suited for anti-oppressive education. That is, the natural sciences can be ideally suited to reveal the ways in which nothing—not knowledge, reasoning, even the concept of "nature" itself—is separable from social institutions, ideologies, and histories. All of science is already framed by certain stories, and these stories often reinforce oppressions circulating in society.

It should be reiterated that critiquing the partial nature of the sciences does not mean that we reject all that the sciences have to offer. The sciences have indeed helped us to improve the quality of life in many ways, and the knowledge that exists in the sciences continues to matter in society today. But the sciences have also had oppressive social, environmental, and bodily consequences. This should not be surprising, given that the sciences are necessarily partial: They cannot help but consist of certain people making certain choices, intentionally or not, about what and how to research in the natural world and how to present these findings. Rather than reject the sciences, I am advocating an approach that examines and raises questions about the underlying stories in the sciences, and their political implications.

Of course, the stories we need to examine are not only those within the sciences, but also those *about* the sciences that circulate in society. When I concluded my lesson in the student-teaching seminar, I asked students to reflect on concerns they would have about teaching the sciences in this way. My students voiced most concern about the ways their students have already learned to think about the sciences that might get in the way of either learning the sciences or learning to critique the sciences. For example, they imagined that some of their students might already distrust the sciences because they believe it contradicts their religious ideas about history, spirituality, and the universe. Or some students might already dismiss critiques of the sciences because they believe that those who are voicing the critiques are radical activists merely trying to advance their own agenda of environmental conservation, gay rights, or redistributing of funds for health services for women or people of color. What students have already learned can significantly influence their openness to learning the sciences in anti-oppressive ways.

Furthermore, this openness or resistance that students consciously or subconsciously feel to learning the sciences can be magnified when the teacher's identities or political commitments are visible. Students who already believe that the sciences contradict Christian teachings might feel even more distrustful if their teacher is not Christian. Students who already dismiss critiques of the sciences might feel that their feminist or anti-racist teacher (or simply female or of-color teacher) is yet another example of a teacher who fails to teach without bias. The identities and life experiences of students and teachers matter when learning the sciences and when learning to critique the sciences. Thus, my students wondered, How, as teachers, do they address these factors?

Their concerns pointed to a shortcoming of my own teaching, namely, my implication that an analysis of underlying stories in the sciences can take place at a purely abstract, rational, depersonalized level. By not asking my students to reflect on what stories they have already learned about the sciences, and what those stories indirectly told them about the trustworthiness of their teacher, I was perhaps ignoring the ways that those stories or our identities mattered in our lesson.

I acknowledged to my students that teachers and students will always be carrying stories about the sciences and predispositions to trusting (or not trusting) the teacher and to learning (or not learning) the sciences and critiques of the sciences. But this should not suggest that our response should be to try to ignore (as I did) or overpower these stories and predispositions. Rather, perhaps our job as teachers is to make these stories and predispositions part of the lesson. We might ask, How do we already think about the sciences? Why do we already feel open to learning only certain aspects of the sciences (or why do we already feel open to learning only certain critiques of the sciences)?

Furthermore, and perhaps more important, how do these stories and predispositions parallel the stories and predispositions that currently govern science communities? That is, just as we are more open to learning only certain things, how might many in science communities be more open to addressing only certain issues, asking only certain questions, using only certain methods, communicating only certain findings? What social forces might encourage this openness to only certain things (such as when funds support only certain areas of research, or discrimination prevents certain groups from entering science communities in significant numbers)? Where might we turn to imagine very different ways of doing science? Exposing and raising questions about the openness and resistance that students feel toward the sciences and toward critiques of the sciences can be a useful way to raise parallel questions about the oppressive tendencies and anti-oppressive possibilities of the people who populate the science communities.

QUESTIONS FOR REFLECTION AND DISCUSSION

1. (Comprehension) What does the invisibility of intersexed bodies in the science curriculum teach us about the relationship between science and "common sense?" What are examples of other stories (gendered or otherwise) that frame how we think and talk about scientific issues?
2. (Concretization) How might you design a lesson that not only teaches a scientific concept, but also teaches the framing of the concept and the possible uses or implications of that concept socially or politically?
3. (Critique) What are examples in history and even today of scientific practices and even of research questions that privilege some groups over others?

SAMPLING OF NEW RESOURCES

For analyses of science education:

- Calabrese Barton, A. (2003). *Teaching Science for Social Justice.* New York: Teachers College Press.
- *Malama I Ka 'Aina:* Culturally Relevant Professional Development. http://malama.hawaii.edu
- *National Girls Collaborative Project:* Women and Girls in STEM. http://www.aauw.org/education/ngcp/index.cfm
- Roth, W.-M., van Eijck, M., Reis, G., & Hsu, P.-L. (2008). *Authentic Science Revisited: In Praise of Diversity, Heterogeneity, Hybridity.* Rotterdam, The Netherlands: Sense Publishers.

11

EXAMPLES FROM MATHEMATICS

More than any other discipline, math is considered by many people to be the least influenced by social factors and, therefore, to be the most bias-free of all subjects being taught and learned in school. People have told me that race might matter when treating students of color differently in a math classroom, but race has little, if anything, to do with adding and subtracting numbers. Unlike the situation in English classes where the racial identity of the author might matter, or in social studies classes where racial identities might affect the experiences of different groups in history, in math classes such differences do not change the value of numbers or the principles of calculating with numbers. The principles behind working with numbers remain true no matter who is doing the work, even in cultures where the numbers and principles may be called different things.

Fortunately, more and more math teachers are recognizing that what and how we teach are influenced by social factors and do have hidden messages that often reinforce oppression. For example, some teachers are recognizing that the wording of word problems can reinforce White-privilege, traditional gender roles, or heterosexism. Therefore, they are changing the language and examples they use to reflect a wider variety of social identities and situations. Some teachers are recognizing that the contexts (textbooks, projects) in which they expect students to learn math often imply that math has little relevance to the lives of the students, and therefore they are emphasizing ways that math can be a tool to understand or make changes in our daily lives or communities. Some teachers are recognizing that ignoring how other cultures have developed different methods of arithmetic and measurement can indirectly teach students that the methods learned in school are the only or the best methods. Such teachers are introducing students to aspects of math that have been developed and used in cultures around the world. Some teachers are even recognizing that students come to school having already learned certain ways of thinking about numbers, and just as students from certain cultural backgrounds have learned to communicate in ways that differ from what is expected in school, so too have students from certain cultural backgrounds learned to think numerically in ways that differ from what is expected in school. Such teachers are finding ways to build from what students already know, not only to value their unique knowledge, but also to show that while there may be ways of thinking numerically that matter in school, there do exist alternative and equally valid ways to think numerically.

What and how we teach can reinforce and/or challenge oppression, including when we try to teach without bias. This should not be surprising. Intentionally or not, schools make choices all the time about what and how they will and will not teach: Which properties of arithmetic, which formulas in algebra, which theorems in geometry, and for that matter, which type of geometry, and in which context, and for what purpose. Textbooks, for example, consist of only certain topics, placed in a certain order, described in only certain ways, illustrated with only certain examples, and applied to only certain contexts and problems. Of course, it is impossible to teach students about every way of thinking mathematically, not only because we are limited by time, but also because there are ways of thinking that we have yet to discover or develop. The problem, however, is not that math curriculum is partial; rather, the problem is that schools do not often make explicit its partial nature. Schools do not make explicit the ways that what is included in math curriculum often reinforces oppression in invisible ways. Instead, schools often teach that there is a correct way to think numerically and that this correct way gives us an unbiased understanding of the world. This notion that math is bias-free is one reason why math curriculum can uniquely contribute to anti-oppressive education. It can teach that even those things we often consider to be abstract and separable from the social and material world (including numbers, algorithms, and mathematical reasoning) cannot help but be taught in ways that have varying political implications.

REAL-LIFE PROBLEMS, REAL LIMITATIONS

I once taught a year-long high school course that combined algebra, trigonometry, and statistics. Each quarter, in an attempt to help students make connections between what they were learning and their everyday lives, I assigned a project in which students were to apply some of the concepts they had just learned. During the first quarter, one of our topics was finding the terms of a function (such as a line or a U-shaped parabola) that could best describe a given set of data. For their project, I asked students to form groups and choose a real-life topic to research that they found interesting and meaningful. They were to write a brief questionnaire that could produce the kind of data needed for this assignment (namely, quantifiable data with two variables), survey a small number of their schoolmates, quantify and chart their results, determine which of the methods learned in class could help them describe their data in the form of a function, and then determine the terms of that function. One group wanted to compare the average number of hours that students spent weekly on math homework with their grades on their most recent exam. They determined that the two variables (homework hours and overall grade) had somewhat of a linear relationship in their data, and they calculated the formula for their "line of best fit." Another group wanted to compare the number of times (out of a set number of tries) that students could shoot a basketball into the hoop with the number of feet away from the hoop that the students stood. They determined the relationship to be somewhat hyperbolic (with significant differences in the first few feet and smaller and smaller differences as the shooters got farther and farther away) and derived a formula accordingly.

Despite my enthusiasm (and perhaps to temper my enthusiasm), students quite vocally complained each time I assigned a project: It was not in the textbook; their friends in classes with other math teachers did not have a project *every* quarter; I was requiring them to write an essay, but ours was not an English class. Yet, many students seemed more excited when working on their projects than when working on the "regular" work. Students would heatedly debate what to select as their group's topic, or how to graph their data, or how to "describe" it with a function. Other teachers would ask me what my students were doing, since the students' research often generated curiosity and discussion among other students (especially when shooting basketballs was part of math homework). Perhaps most important, some students would write in their course evaluations that the "extra" work of the projects was the most engaging thing we did all quarter, or they would say that, more than my review sessions, it made the concepts concrete and doable, and for that matter, connected to their lives. The feedback from my students convinced me that I was at least somewhat successful in achieving my goals of engaging students and making math meaningful, all while enhancing students' abilities to learn and apply what they were learning.

Why is this significant? Because all too often, math is not taught in ways that all students find meaningful and relevant to their lives, and as a result, certain groups of students have traditionally been disadvantaged in math classes, including female students and students of color. In my class of predominantly female students of color, I took some comfort knowing that I was not contributing to an oppressive pattern too often seen in math classes. By teaching and learning math within the context of solving a problem or answering a question that students found meaningful, we were able to make math more "real" and, thus, more engaging. Making such connections is certainly a goal of the national standards now driving math education in the United States.

As I look back on my course, I realize that there are additional ways that I could have challenged oppression. For example, I could have asked students to find examples of when people in society have advanced oppressive or anti-oppressive causes by using the math that my students had just used in their own projects. After all, math is used all the time in society to address various social problems, support various claims, or advocate for various changes. We use math when we determine what a school needs, what a community wants, or what a district looks like. We depend on math to tell us which group is succeeding, which group is growing, which group deserves our limited resources. And we often conclude that this presumably bias-free method of mathematical analysis justifies adopting certain policies, selecting certain curriculum, and distributing resources in certain ways.

Why is this a problem? Because math is not bias-free. We use math in ways that cannot help but to be influenced by countless assumptions and choices, often in oppressive ways. We might determine that a school needs more resources for its growing population of students with limited English-language skills and not determine that it also needs resources to curb the rapidly growing number of homophobic incidents because questions on homophobia were not even on the survey. We might determine that a community wants more resources for athletics without realizing that those who voted for more athletics suspected that the people conducting the survey were more willing to give funds for athletics than for what the majority really wanted, which was a larger arts program. We might determine that Asian Americans are doing "better" than other racial groups in our schools because their cultural heritage values education, without our realizing that the research question itself ("why are they doing better?") already assumes that Asian Americans are actually doing better in education. Furthermore, we might determine that, because Asian Americans are doing "better" in education, our affirmative action policy does not need to target them, without realizing that certain Asian American ethnic groups actually fare very poorly in school compared to the national norm. Without interpreting math in a critical way, such underlying assumptions and choices may never be unearthed, and the political implications, never challenged.

I did not ask my students to reflect on these implications in larger society (such as when reading polls, measurements, statistics, and so forth in the news media). I did not even ask my students to reflect on these implications in their own projects. I do not remember problematizing the math that the students were learning. Consider the group that compared hours of homework with grades on exams. We did not discuss how a research question cannot be asked without making a range of assumptions and choices and without some expectations, including the assumption that no other factors will influence the relationship between hours and grades, the assumption that interviewees will know the number of hours they study and report it truthfully to the interviewer, the assumption that exams were graded fairly or at least in a manner consistent across the interviewees, the choice of exam grades instead of quarter grades, the choice of homework instead of groupwork, the expectation that exams should reflect what was learned, the expectation that homework should help students learn, and the expectation that more time on homework means more learning.

We did not discuss how the methods of data collection can influence the data collected, including how the questions were worded, whether the surveys were administered privately and confidentially, what the relationship was like between the interviewers and the interviewees, and how the interviewees were selected. We did not discuss how the methods of data summary can influence the results, including how the data are charted or graphed, how the function is determined, how the terms of the function are determined, or simply why only certain types of charts and functions are acceptable results. We did not discuss how the methods of data analysis cannot be conducted without bias from the researcher: how the interpretation of the results is influenced by the researchers' values and perspectives, or how different interpretations are more or less likely because of researchers' different life experiences and previous knowledge. We did not discuss the history of the math that they were learning, and ways that mathematicians have made choices and assumptions to arrive at those theories or concepts. We did not discuss reasons why those theories and concepts are the ones that seem to matter in schools and society. We did not discuss ways that other mathematicians have critiqued such theories or concepts.

We certainly did not discuss alternative methods for analyzing the situation or problem, and the different political implications of such alternatives. Nor did we discuss how math, like any other discipline, often tells us only certain stories about the world, especially stories that have traditionally been privileged in society. For example, we often learn that math is a tool to understand the world objectively, to provide *a* correct answer to our questions. True, there may be different paths to arrive at that answer, and there may be different real-life implications of the answer, and teachers often do encourage students to explore these different paths and implications, but the answer itself is clear and unambiguous. It is often a number or a formula. Unlike the results of literary analysis or historical research, math presumes to get rid of "subjective" matters by quantifying the world around us, thus producing an understanding of the world that can be represented with neutral symbols and principals. Math not only simplifies the world, but also does so in ways that tell the correct story. This simplification happens even when studying complexity and chaos, since the goal is often to find patterns in what we generally consider to be irreducible and unpredictable.

I do not mean to suggest that simplifying the world is not helpful or useful. In many ways, we need to be able to measure things, to describe things, to summarize things, to predict things. However, we also need to acknowledge that any way of simplifying the world makes possible only certain insights into what it could mean to address such problems as social conflicts, environmental destruction, and physiological illness. In fact, we need to acknowledge that the very process of simplifying the world can make challenging oppression difficult for those who believe it is important to understand the world in terms of the subjective, non-quantifiable, social aspects of who we are and how we live. Unfortunately, all too often, schools do not teach about how math often socializes students into thinking about the world in only certain, presumably bias-free ways. Math is often treated as a neutral tool that, once mastered, can be used to objectively understand our world.

It is not surprising, then, that most of my students did not think it necessary to raise questions about the historical influences, personal assumptions, and political implications involved in the mathematical analyses they undertook for their projects. To conclude their projects, I had students write essays to describe their topics, methods, and results, as well as to reflect on the limitations of their projects. Some students did discuss the limitations in terms of the ways their results could have been influenced by how they worded their questions or by the lack of confidentiality in their surveys. But most did not. Most students focused on their inability to work as a group or their procrastination and sloppiness. Students generally seemed to understand "limitations" in terms of what got in the way of their doing the math properly, as if the math itself were not, in some ways, partial. I suspect that a hidden message in my teaching likely repeated the message we often hear about math, namely, that it produces knowledge of the world free of social and political aspects. I suspect, in other words, that I reinforced the commonsensical notion that math, if done correctly, really can be bias-free.

LOOKING BEYOND: INSTITUTIONAL DEMANDS

I once described these reflections on an anti-oppressive approach to math education in my seminar for student teachers. Although many of them supported the idea that teaching math should include teaching to think critically about math, they also wondered how possible such an approach would be, given the schools' demands to document what students have learned in quantifiable ways. They wondered, What would it mean to assess and evaluate student learning in such a class? What would it mean to score or grade such learning? Do grades even belong in anti-oppressive education?

Earlier in the seminar, we had discussed my own concerns about how to grade them. I had shared with my students my feelings that grades are inherently problematic. Different teachers grade differently, making it difficult to compare grades from different students and different teachers. But even when different teachers grade consistently, grades cannot help but be influenced significantly by what students learned or did not learn before even beginning a course. This is the case even when grading from portfolios, or by standards, or through self-assessments. Some students already know certain mathematical concepts taught in school or are already familiar with the language, examples, manipulatives, and situations we often use to teach or illustrate math. Some students have already learned how to study and complete their homework properly. Some students already know what gets rewarded during class discussions or what is expected when taking notes during lectures. Some students already know how to figure out what teachers want to hear repeated in exams, and feel comfortable taking paper-and-pencil exams. Some students already know, in other words, what it takes to get a high grade in class, and these students are often those who have traditionally been privileged in schools.

Teachers do not always begin the school year teaching to all students these skills and assumptions and rules for learning and demonstrating what has been learned. Without learning these tacit rules, some students will not succeed, regardless of their abilities and regardless of what they actually end up learning. What students bring and do not bring into the classroom matters. Why is this important? Because the grades students end up with are often used to rank and sort them for future schooling and employment. Why should students be rewarded for being fortunate enough for already having learned what matters in school? If grades cannot help but to be influenced by what students already know, why are we continuing to place value on grades? Shouldn't students and teachers alike be learning to raise questions about and resist our taken-for-granted notions of what matters in school?

I told my students that I had these concerns about assignments, and grades, and what they were and were not learning and had and had not already learned. I described my hope that they would determine for themselves what it was that they wanted to get out of my courses, and then work toward those goals. Learning should not be about jumping through the same hoops students have always had to jump through. I made explicit my hope that students would not feel that, to get a good grade, they could or should merely repeat what some in society or even I have said that they needed to know. It is true that I wanted them to learn the knowledge and skills that get rewarded in schools and society (including things that they needed to learn to get certified by the state to teach in public schools). But I also wanted them to learn to raise questions about the political implications of the official knowledge in schools as well as possible alternative ways to understand and live in this world. I wanted students to look beyond what it was that I was teaching.

Ironically, even in my seminar, there were hoops: Students were still required to produce assignments that were to be graded according to criteria I had already delineated. They wondered aloud: Was I really teaching my course in a way informed by these critiques of traditional methods of evaluating and then ranking students? I did have a range of assignments with varied goals and varied means of assessment. I did generally grade very highly, as a way to subvert a system that placed so much value on differentiating students by grades. Yet, I did not completely abandon grades, primarily because we were teaching and learning in a context where grades often did matter: Grades determined who got accepted into the limited space of teacher-certification programs, or who got funded, who got offered a job, and so forth. Social and institutional pressure made it quite difficult to radically change what grades meant in my course or to do away with grades altogether.

I admitted to my students that I was still revising my grading policy and that, in fact, I likely will never reach a point where I will feel that my policy is unproblematic, which means that I was not sure how to suggest they proceed with grading in their own classes, math or otherwise. Complicating matters further, there will likely be institutional demands that make challenging oppression quite difficult. I admitted that these admissions made me a very uncomfortable teacher. Yet, I suggested that perhaps this is what it means to teach in anti-oppressive ways. Perhaps discussing with our students the problems with which we personally struggle as teachers is what can help students to raise critical questions about the partial nature of what and how they are learning.

QUESTIONS FOR REFLECTION AND DISCUSSION

1. (Comprehension) What are various examples of bias in how we teach and learn mathematics in school, as well as how we use or "do" mathematics in research?
2. (Concretization) How might you teach in ways that avoid or challenge these examples of bias? And how might you teach in ways that avoid or challenge the notion that mathematics itself is uninfluenced by social or political factors?
3. (Critique) How would you address the quandaries raised about grading?

SAMPLING OF NEW RESOURCES

For analyses of mathematics education:

- Greer, B., Mukhopadhyay, S., Powell, A., & Nelson-Barber, S. (Eds.). (2009). *Culturally Responsive Mathematics Education*. New York: Routledge.
- Gutstein, E., & Peterson, B. (2005). *Rethinking Mathematics: Teaching Social Justice by the Numbers*. Milwaukee, WI: Rethinking Schools.
- Leonard, J. (2007). *Culturally Specific Pedagogy in the Mathematics Classroom: Strategies for Teachers and Students*. Mahwah, NJ: Lawrence Erlbaum Associates.
- Martin, D. B. (2006). *Mathematics Success and Failure Among African-American Youth: The Roles of Sociohistorical Context, Community Forces, School Influence, and Individual Agency*. Mahwah, NJ: Lawrence Erlbaum.

CONCLUSION: WITH HOPE

It is important that readers not feel discouraged by the never-ending and ever-contradictory nature of anti-oppressive education. Admittedly, anti-oppressive education faces many barriers, both practical and political. Many practical barriers arise from the refusal of these theories to name concrete implications. The notion that anti-oppressive education differs from situation to situation puts much responsibility on teachers to deduce what it means to teach in anti-oppressive ways in this classroom in this moment, versus in that classroom in another moment. The work of applying anti-oppressive perspectives in the classroom is never-ending and, when combined with the insistence that we constantly problematize our own practices (including the practices and perspectives suggested by this book), can weigh heavily on teachers who are already burdened with heavy workloads, low social and economic support, and contradictory demands from parents, colleagues, and supervisors. In addition, teachers committed to anti-oppressive education face political pressure in the form of public bashing, scrutiny from both the Left and the Right, and increasing policy initiatives that require substantial curriculum revisions in the face of high-stakes tests and highly valued "learning standards." Combined with punishments for teachers and schools with low success rates on indicators like student-achievement scores, and the increasing influence of the political and religious Right over school boards, the climate in many schools is not often welcoming or supportive of anti-oppressive changes. So, wherein lies the hope?

A few years ago, I had a student teacher who struggled immensely with classroom management. She found it difficult to keep her mixed-ability classes focused and engaged, and at times the students were quite disrespectful. The student teacher expressed to me her hope that, when teaching full-time, she would be assigned an honors class of students who were mature and engaged enough to make classroom management a nonissue. Such a class, she believed, would be one in which she could really teach. In response, I asked her whether "teaching" was something that happened only when students behaved in certain ways, namely, in ways we often think "good"" students are supposed to behave? Was it a problem, in other words, to think that good classroom management preceded real teaching? Some of the theories we read in class suggested that student engagement can have everything to do with what and how we teach, and in fact, that wanting and expecting students to be students in only certain ways might lie at the heart of teaching "problems."

That same year, I taught a seminar where several student teachers complained that anti-oppressive education seemed impossible. There were so many complexities of oppression, so many contradictions of activism, so many nuances in what and how we teach, and given that even the "expert" (the professor) was still exploring what it could mean to teach in anti-oppressive ways, and given the ways that every approach to anti-oppressive education seemed to have weaknesses, they wondered whether they would ever know enough to teach anti-oppressively. In response, I asked them whether anti-oppressive teaching is something that happens only when all the complexities are known, when all the contradictions are prevented, and when all the weaknesses are addressed? Was it a problem, in other words, to require that teachers come to a full understanding of oppression and teaching before they feel comfortable teaching anti-oppressively? Was it a problem to define anti-oppressive teaching as only those instances of teaching that were fully and unproblematically anti-oppressive? Some of the theories we read in class suggested that anti-oppressive education is not something that happens when the contradictions and partialities are gone, and instead, is exactly what happens when we are working through these "problems." In fact, some of the theories we read in class suggested that approaches to teaching that presume to be unproblematic are the very approaches we want to critique. I wondered aloud: Perhaps it is the expectation that anti-oppressive teaching happens only in ideal situations that makes teaching feel so impossible and suffocating.

Becoming anti-oppressive teachers requires not that we first reach a certain point, or that we first revamp everything about our teaching, or that we step outside of practical and political barriers. Anti-oppressive teaching happens only when we are trying to address the partial nature of our own teaching. As illustrated throughout this book, it happens when we focus on one unit, or one lesson, or one moment of our teaching, and rethink the possibilities for change within the particular social, historical, political, and pedagogical context in which it arose. As educators look to the future, I urge engaging in anti-oppressive education in this step-by-step, lesson-by-lesson manner. Such a process may seem tedious. But to me, such a process is what helps to make teaching exciting, and challenging, and liberating. Such a process is what gives me hope that anti-oppressive education is possible in my own classroom.

Perhaps educators do not often expect that teaching, learning, and learning to teach require doing this kind of work. But then again, challenging oppression requires teaching and learning in very different ways. I hope many educators will find these ideas useful as we prepare more teachers for anti-oppressive education. And I look forward to the changes in our schools and society that result.

SAMPLING OF NEW RESOURCES

For examples of resources for anti-oppressive education across the subject areas and for various age levels:

- Adams, M., Bell, L. A., & Griffin, P. (Eds.). (2007). *Teaching for Diversity and Social Justice*, 2nd Edition. New York: Routledge.
- Au, W. B., Bigelow, B., & Karp, S. (2007). *Rethinking Our Classrooms: Teaching for Equity and Justice*, New Edition. Milwaukee, WI: Rethinking Schools.
- EdChange Multicultural Education Pavilion. http://www.edchange.org/multicultural
- Education for Liberation Network. http://www.edliberation.org
- Educators for Social Responsibility. http://www.esrnational.org
- Encyclopedia of Peace Education. http://www.tc.edu/centers/epe/index.html
- Grant, C. A., & Sleeter, C. E. (2008). *Turning on Learning: Five Approaches for Multicultural Teaching Plans for Race, Class, Gender and Disability*, 5th Edition. New York: John Wiley & Sons, Ltd.
- Mack, T., & Picower, B. (Eds.). (2008). *Planning to Change the World: A Plan Book for Social Justice Teachers*. New York: Justice Plan Books.
- New York Collective of Radical Educators. http://www.nycore.org
- Rethinking Schools (Ed.). (2004). *The New Teacher Book: Finding Purpose, Balance and Hope During Your First Years in the Classroom*. Milwaukee, WI: Rethinking Schools.

AFTERWORD

Kevin Kumashiro began his teaching career, as did many others: he wanted to "help." He joined the Peace Corps and was assigned to Nepal where he realized that the Peace Corps relied on a commonsensical definition of good teaching, a culturally specific definition, namely, one informed by how teaching was practiced in the United States. Kumashiro is critical of the Peace Corps' failure to critique its unspoken assumptions about U.S. superiority. "Good teaching" is not, he observes, a neutral concept.

His experience in the Peace Corps underscored for Kumashiro the limits of common sense. "Oppression is masked by or couched in concepts that make us think that this is the way things are supposed to be," he observes, a point made by Michael Moriarty (1991, 36) in a different context: "Coercion is camouflaged as the statement of the obvious." "Common sense," Kumashiro concurs, "does not often tell us that the status quo is quite oppressive. . . . And it rarely tells us that schools need to place a priority on challenging oppression." Oppression is a plural noun, he points out; it is multiple in nature. And anti-oppressive education draws upon multiple traditions, among them feminist, critical, multicultural, queer, and postcolonial traditions, as well as other movements toward social justice.

Working toward social justice requires anti-oppressive teaching. No teacher education program, Kumashiro reports, requires significant coursework in critical perspectives, such as multicultural critiques of mathematics, feminist histories of the natural sciences, postcolonial perspectives on English literature, and queer re-readings of history. Moreover, almost no programs make central the study of anti-oppressive methods that focused on differences, equity, power, and oppression. Kumashiro comments:

> It is certainly important that teachers try to know their students, know their subjects, and know how to teach, and programs should continue to ensure that teachers are learned in these ways. However, it is equally important that teachers know the limits of their knowledge.

Kumashiro understands that the hegemony of academic psychology in many schools and departments of education limit the ways prospective and practicing teachers can understand themselves and their students. This point—made compellingly by Dwayne Huebner (1999 [1966]) almost forty years ago—is reiterated by Kumashiro: "Psychological models are not the only ways to know our students, and different models or lenses can lead to different insights. It is problematic, then, to privilege only certain (psychological) ways of knowing students." The reification of psychological constructs—such as "skills"—has done much to damage our capacity to think creatively about education.

The obnoxious demand for "standards" (as if teachers had not had them before) is, among other things (such as the erasure of academic, i.e., intellectual, freedom), a suppression of creativity. As Kumashiro observes, "Learning to standards in the disciplines is a practice of repetition, of repeating or perpetuating only certain ways of knowing or doing the disciplines." In this regard, "standards" tend to obscure the dynamism of the disciplines, including their own interdisciplinary tendencies, and their profoundly historical and political character. Kumashiro does not fail to make this last point, noting that "since any perspective or practice is partial, learning to standards is a practice that reinforces the privilege of only certain perspectives and groups in society."

When teacher education attends to "standards," then, it betrays the very disciplines the idea presumably honors. And by their bureaucratization, "standards" standardize and bureaucratize the school subjects as they impoverish, intellectually, academic education courses. Certainly they denude many university-based courses of any "critical" content. As Kumashiro reports, "Almost no [teacher education] program made central use of readings and assignments on anti-oppressive methods that focused on differences, equity, power, and oppression." What would attention to these subjects require?

TROUBLING KNOWLEDGE

First and foremost, attention to these subjects would require "troubling knowledge," by which Kumashiro means "to complicate knowledge, to make knowledge problematic." The emphasis here is on the gerund. "Troubling" means

> to work paradoxically with knowledge, to simultaneously see what different insights, identities, practices, and changes it makes possible while critically examining that knowledge (and how it came to be known) to see what insights and the like it closes off.

Second, by "troubling knowledge" Kumashiro means knowledge that is "disruptive, discomforting, problematizing." Focusing on the noun, he asks for curriculum that is unfamiliar, does not coincide with commonsensical understandings, and that disrupts taken-for-granted conceptions of what is. Becoming a practitioner of troubling knowledge, then, can never be about "mastery or full knowledge; the goal can never be to fill that partiality and erase the politics." Nor can we assume that troubling knowledge is a "better" body of knowledge, since, as he points out, "any body of knowledge is partial." "Rather," he continues (and here is the core of his conception), "the goal is to examine the different uses and effects of different bodies of knowledge, and explore the anti-oppressive changes made possible from them." This means that "learning to teach in anti-oppressive ways also needs to involve examining how 'good' teaching can be problematic."

"An anti-oppressive teacher is not something that someone is," Kumashiro asserts. "Rather, it is something that someone is always becoming." Why? First, the practices of anti-oppressive teaching require constant problematization: "No practice, in and of itself, is anti-oppressive." Second, mainstream conceptions of what it means to be a teacher do not often include anti-oppressive roles and responsibilities. The identity of "anti-oppressive" teacher is "paradoxical," Kumashiro concludes, because an "anti-oppressive teacher is always trying to change what it means to be a teacher. The teacher is always becoming anti-oppressive but never fully is." The point is not to fix the identity of "teacher." That identity is always situated, in flux, ever-changing, always critical.

Teachers and students often resist such "paradoxical" understandings of their roles and responsibilities, desiring fixed, authoritative positions. Resistance and desire are, Kumashiro asserts, "central to the process of learning," even in learning to challenge oppression. "The reason we are not doing more to challenge oppression," he suggests, "is not merely that we do not know enough about oppression, but also that we often do not *want* to know more about oppression." As a consequence, resistance and desire ought not be disdained or denied as "hindrances," and thereby suppressed or ignored or overpowered. Rather, resistance and desire should become part of what students study: "Students' desire for and resistances to learning need to become part of what they are learning." In terms of challenging oppression," he suggests, "it would also be important to address the political, social, *emotional* reasons why oppression so often plays out invisibly and unchallenged in our lives."

There is smart discussion of "learning through crisis," wherein Kumashiro notes, with the voice of experience perhaps, that "crisis can lead a student to desire change, but it can lead a student to resist change even more strongly than before." Consequently, "when students are in a state of crisis, teachers need to structure experiences that can help students to work through it." Moreover: "Learning through crisis is not a process that can be standardized for all students."

In order to prepare teachers for uncertainty, "maybe we need to start feeling very uncomfortable about the processes of teaching and learning." Gender is a case in point, as he recognizes that "the intentional lessons on gender stand little chance in countering the unintentional ones." In this sense, teaching is "impossible." Kumashiro continues:

> Yes, teaching is impossible, but only if we believe that teaching is successful when student learn exactly what we said beforehand that they were supposed to learn. Were we to define teaching as a process that not only gives students the knowledge and skills that matter in society, but also asks students to examine the political implications of that knowledge and skills, then we should expect that there will always be more to our teaching than what we intended.

The point, he suggests, "is to conscientiously make visible these hidden lessons and the various lenses being used by students to make sense of them."

Kumashiro expresses his "profound discomfort at the idea that there are 'foundations' to teacher education and that through the required set of courses, all student teachers will learn these foundations." Like other fields, he suggests, "teacher education ... does not seem to acknowledge the partial nature of what it requires students to learn, and in doing so, often remains disconnected from the everyday lived realities of students." To explore the possibility of connection, he asks: "What might socially engaged Buddhism tell us about teaching and learning against oppression?" To answer, he draws upon Nhat Hanh, for whom learning is not equivalent to the acquisition of more knowledge. "Learning," Kumashiro tells us,

> is about releasing our dependence on knowledge that has, until now, framed the ways we live in this world. In other words, central to the processes of teaching and learning is addressing the imitations of how we teach and learn and what we know and are coming to know.

Such a process is not primarily psychological, nor is it expressed in self-reflection; it is a matter of activism.

Kumashiro asks us to think about preparing teachers for activism. To do so, he offers "a reflection on things queer." Just as his discussion of Buddhism is no argument to teach students to be Buddhist, so too his discussion of queer activism is no argument that we should be teaching students to be sexually queer. Rather, reflecting on queer activism enables him to ask: "What would happen if we explored approaches to social justice that were premised on being uncomfortable?" While "not the answer to our problems," Kumashiro suggests, "queer activism can suggest ways of thinking that go beyond common sense." It requires us to ask: "What is problematic with the norm?" He concludes: "Like queer activism, queer teaching always works *through* crisis."

To illustrate how such teaching might work in the current curriculum, Kumashiro focuses on one topic within several of the school subjects. He has no intention of presenting "*the* anti-oppressive way to think about and teach these discipline," or how "to revise the entire curriculum within a discipline." "Rarely," he confides, "have these reflections on my lessons left me content with my teaching."

While endorsing curriculum change in literature courses— "more and more educators are recognizing that teaching and learning English literature in ways that challenge oppression requires changing what we read"—he does not assume that reading multicultural literature is unproblematic: "Some writings can merely repeat stereotypes or create new ones by glossing over complexities, contradictions, and diversity, thereby suggesting that an entire culture or a group is *like this*."

Moreover, exploring issues of identification and dis-identification with characters in multicultural literature does not necessarily change how students think about themselves. He notes that the "classics" are not necessarily oppressive. Much would seem to depend on how they are taught, and Kumashiro asks that teachers critique their own "lenses" for reading and teaching texts, requiring of them, he suggests, "a level of vulnerability that we do not often expect in the classroom." "[P]erhaps," he offers, "this modeling of self-critique can be exactly what helps students to look beyond the lesson." He continues:

> In fact, sometimes when teachers raise questions about their own cultural assumptions, they can model the kind of self-critique and vulnerability that they invite their students to experience. Teachers could show that even teachers have work to do when challenging the norms that govern our lives.

Kumashiro began this book critiquing the Peace Corps' cultural imperialism, a critique he was able to make, in part, through his experiences growing up in Hawai'i. He points out that "Christian missionaries worked to help 'them' be more like 'us,' and in this case, to educate Hawaiians in the ways that 'Americans' are educated and to get Hawaiians to worship in the ways that Protestant Americans worship." He reports that it was not until "well beyond my elementary school years that I noticed that the lyrics of my favorite Hawaiian song centered on a Christian theme." To help students to "look beyond" the lesson and learn in "anti-oppressive ways," teachers might, for instance, point out that Hawai'i is not only a tropical paradise, but also a site "of domination and racism against which people have long struggled and continue to struggle."

Such a lesson provides little comfort for the teacher working against oppression, as there is the danger, Kumashiro points out, that "teaching about differences can further objectify the Other." He seems to suggest that this danger is moderated when lessons focus on both "self and other." "Fortunately," he writes, "lessons about other cultures do not have to teach only about the Other. It can also teach about ourselves." In the chapter on teaching "foreign" languages in anti-oppressive ways, he notes that our aspiration involves "changing our ideas about and relationships with others. But it also involves changing our ideas and feelings about ourselves."

Contesting the academic vocationalism that currently structures curricula in the natural sciences, Kumashiro advocates becoming literate and savvy regarding the social, political, and cultural consequences of those fields. In sync with the work of poststructuralist theoreticians such as Michel Serres and Bruno Latour, Kumashiro suggests that it is important that students learn that "we are using different stories to understand the world, that different stories have different political implications, and that the stories currently framing the natural sciences do indeed have oppressive implications for U.S. society."

To illustrate, Kumashiro focuses on gender, specifically on the ideology of "opposite sexes." "Of course, this binary, hierarchical story is not the only way to understand gender," he notes, and "throughout history, other cultures in this world have indeed understood gender in different ways." But in the contemporary science curriculum, this ideology often passes for science. Acknowledging that there is a continuum of possible genders, that "gender" can be an ambiguous conception (he cites intersexed births), makes less likely naïve assertions of gender and sexuality. Acknowledging that there are more than two genders, he continues, "makes it difficult to assert that we are supposed to be sexually attracted only to members of the 'opposite gender.'"

Not only science is presented as apolitical and beyond culture in the current school curriculum. Kumashiro reminds us: "Math is often treated as a neutral tool that, once mastered, can be used to objectively understand our world." The educational point is that "students need to be examining the underlying stories of the curriculum and the ways that the stories can both reinforce and challenge oppression." This "never-ending and ever-contradictory nature of anti-oppressive education," Kumashiro allows, can seem discouraging. Anti-oppressive education faces many barriers, "both practical and political."

To illustrate the "practical," Kumashiro focuses on classroom management. For many teachers, "good classroom management precede[s] real teaching." Kumashiro reminds us that anti-oppressive education does not occur "only when all the complexities are known, when all the contradictions are prevented, and when all the weaknesses are addressed." Anti-oppressive education, it is clear, occurs as we articulate complexities, work the contradictions, and acknowledge weaknesses. "As educators look to the future," Kumashiro, with a hopefulness I think few feel but which all will welcome, writes:

> I urge engaging in anti-oppressive education in this step-by-step, lesson-by-lesson manner. Such a process may seem tedious. But to me, such a process is what helps to make teaching exciting, and challenging, and liberating. Such a process is what gives me hope that anti-oppressive education is possible in my own classroom.

While the academic—intellectual—freedom educators enjoy in their own classrooms contracts in standardized examination-driven curricula, that freedom can only be claimed by those who can work the complexities, the contradictions, and weaknesses of those ever-changing spaces of the classroom. "Plain talk" to teachers is more urgent than ever, and I thank Kevin Kumashiro for contributing significantly to such conversation.

There has been an ongoing debate over whether or not such "plain talk" is possible. Some have argued that "theory" is necessarily removed from the conditions of the classroom; others have insisted that such remove is "elitist" and that those of us located in the academy must abandon theory in order to address questions of practice. It seems to me that Kumashiro has settled this debate. His book is a sophisticated, nuanced work of "theory" that clearly and accessibly addresses the practical problems of the classroom teacher.

The conditions of public education today are oppressive. The hour is late and the sense of emergency acute. Amidst the maelstrom of the present, the calm, clear, and unwavering voice of Kevin Kumashiro is very much needed. It is incumbent upon us teacher educators to offer this voice to our students. Kumashiro appreciates that we are key; he says so simply, humbly, but with confidence:

> I hope many educators will find these ideas useful as we prepare more teachers for anti-oppressive education. And I look forward to the changes in our schools and society that result.

So do I.

REFERENCES

Huebner, Dwayne E. (1966). Curricular language and classroom meanings. In James B. Macdonald & Robert Leeper (Eds.), *Language and Meaning* (8-26). Washington, DC: Association for Supervision and Curriculum Development. Reprinted in Dwayne E. Huebner, (1999). *The Lure of the Transcendent: Collected Essays.* Edited by Vikki Hillis. [Collected and introduced by William F. Pinar.] Mahwah, NJ: Lawrence Erlbaum.

Moriarty, Michael. (1991). *Roland Barthes.* Stanford, CA: Stanford University Press.

William F. Pinar
Lousiana State University

INDEX

('i' indeicates an illustration; 't' indicates a table)